MW00559069

DREAM GOLF COURSES

A FIREFLY BOOK

Published by Firefly Books Ltd. 2023
Designed and produced by olo.éditions
© 2020, olo.éditions, Paris
© 2020, Éditions Gründ, a department of Édi8, for the French edition.

All rights reserved. No part of this publication may be reproduced,
stored in a retrieval system, or transmitted in any form or by any
means, electronic, mechanical, photocopying, recording or otherwise,
without the prior written permission of the Publisher.

First printing

Library of Congress Control Number: 2023936274

Library and Archives Canada Cataloguing in Publication
Title: Dream golf courses : remarkable golf courses around the world /
    Christophe Thoreau.
Other titles: Plus beaux endroits pour golfer. English
Names: Thoreau, Christophe, author.
Description: Translation of: Les plus beaux endroits pour golfer.
Identifiers: Canadiana 20230223656 | ISBN 9780228104162 (hardcover)
Subjects: LCSH: Golf courses—Pictorial works. | LCSH: Golf courses. |
    LCGFT: Illustrated works.
Classification: LCC GV975 .T56 2023 | DDC 796.35206/8—dc23

Published in Canada by
Firefly Books Ltd.
50 Staples Avenue, Unit 1
Richmond Hill, Ontario
L4B 0A7

Published in the United States by
Firefly Books (U.S.) Inc.
P.O. Box 1338, Ellicott Station
Buffalo, New York
14205

Translations: Travod International Ltd.

Printed in China

Front cover: Lofoten Links, Norway.
Back cover: Île aux Cerfs Golf Club, Mauritius; Emirates Golf Club,
United Arab Emirates; Royal Hawaiian Golf Club, United States.

CHRISTOPHE **THOREAU**

DREAM GOLF COURSES

REMARKABLE GOLF COURSES AROUND THE WORLD

FIREFLY BOOKS

n 1971, during the Apollo 14 lunar landing mission, astronaut Alan Shepard took his 6-iron and played a few shots on the moon. This famous scene did a great deal for the image of a sport that was seen by many people at the time as conservative and snobbish.

Some 50 years later, there are an estimated 35,000 golf courses around the world. With more than 60 million club members worldwide, golf has become the most popular individual sport on the planet. We are witnessing the democratization and globalization of a sport that has its roots in 16th-century Scotland, specifically St. Andrews, where golf was born and which now hosts thousands of golf enthusiasts every year.

This process has been accelerated by the expansion of the professional circuit since the 1970s, the extensive television coverage of events and the popularity of players like Jack Nicklaus and Tiger Woods, just two of the many modern players who are now household names.

Golf is steeped in the most remarkable history and traditions. It is a way of life that offers a sense of community and, above all, an opportunity to be at one with nature. It has found a home amidst some of the most outstanding landscapes on the planet, enhancing the enjoyment of playing amid unceasing wonders and providing a magnificent sense of freedom and release.

The aim of this book is to showcase some of the best, most beautiful and most original golf courses around the world. Swinging at Cape Kidnappers, New Zealand; chipping at Lofoten, Norway; putting at Old Head, Ireland; escaping a bunker at Hirono, Japan; and getting out of the rough at Sperone, France, are moments without parallel. Walking in the footsteps of the game's greatest players across championship courses like Pebble Beach, United States, and Carnoustie, Scotland, is exhilarating, as is dreaming of playing those wonderful but still private courses. For clubs like Seminole, United States, and Shanqin Bay, China, the fact that it is so difficult for mere mortals to get inside simply enhances their legendary status and adds to the mystique that surrounds them.

In the era of climate change, the golfing community must continue their pursuit of more sustainable approaches. We must never forget that we owe golf's magnificence to the wonders this Earth gives us.

If you're not at St. Andrews for its courses, then you might be among the 42% of the town's population who attends the University of St. Andrews, one of the world's most prestigious colleges, founded in 1413. However, a different story began here back in the 16th century, with the creation of the game that would eventually become golf. St. Andrews would go on to become the mecca of golf, with its six courses in addition to the Old Course. The New Course is another very high level links course. The Castle Course dates from 2008 and is located on a cliff top overlooking the city. The Jubilee Course was designed in the 19th century for ladies and beginners and would undergo layout changes and become a championship course in 1988. The Eden Course dates from 1914 and is more forgiving but riddled with bunkers. The Strathtyrum has only 15 holes but is famous for its tough greens. Finally, the Balgove is a nine-hole family course open to beginners and children. At St. Andrews, golf is a religion — everyone gets involved!

Established
1552

Par
72

Length (from the back tees)
7,305 yards
(6,680 m)

Green fees*
US $123–247
*Additional fees subject to change.

St. Andrews Links *St. Andrews, Scotland*

While tennis fans head to Wimbledon and soccer enthusiasts dream of magical evenings at Rio's Maracaña, every year thousands of golf lovers converge on what is thought to be the oldest golf club in the world: St. Andrews. They come to take on one of the seven public courses at the "Home of Golf" and set foot on the most prestigious of them all, the Old Course, which hosts the British Open. This links course, designed by Allan Robertson and Old Tom Morris, is open to amateurs, but you'll need a bit of luck too. Since demand is so high, only the chosen few, picked at random, get to play there. Two-time winner in 1970 and 1978 Jack Nicklaus "fell in love with it" the first time he played there! The American champion mastered this course, which is often battered by gales blowing in off the North Sea and provides unexpected bounces and extremely wide greens, sometimes making putts of 20 yards or more a necessity. However, what makes the Old Course really special is its 112 pot bunkers, which are often so deep as to be unplayable, like the Hell Bunker in the middle of the 14th fairway. The course's highlight is its world-famous 17th hole. A par 4 with a narrow and bumpy fairway, you need to watch out for the Road Hole Bunker, which has brought many dreams to an abrupt end. Even the greatest players have struggled to make par on the 17th hole...

St. Andrews Links *St. Andrews, Scotland*

"For souls nobly born, valor doesn't await the passing of years…" The words of Corneille could have been written about Kingsbarns, which prides itself on being the only modern Scottish links course able to compete with the institutions of St. Andrews and Carnoustie. Although this young club only turned 20 in 2020, historians believe that the first balls were struck here back in 1793. The land then went through several changes. The course was turned into farmland before being requisitioned by the army after the Second World War. It was finally transformed back into greens and fairways at the dawn of the 21st century thanks to the talent of Kyle Phillips. The US architect took inspiration from different links courses, including Royal Dornoch, to develop the most natural course and layout possible. The result is a course that looks as if it has been created by Mother Nature herself, despite the hundreds of thousands of tons of earth that were shifted, piled up and reshaped to hug the coastline and give players unobstructed views of the North Sea.

Established
2000

Par
72

Length
7,223 yards
(6,605 m)

Green fees*
US $191–383
*Additional fees subject to change.

Kingsbarns Golf Links *Kingsbarns, Scotland*

In peak season, the success of Kingsbarns is plain for all to see. Indeed, it is advisable to avoid this course during the summer months, as you risk being hurried along at a furious pace. But how could anyone not want to play on this links course? Though newly created, it's success rivals that of centuries-old venues. Opened in 2000, this course now features in the Dunhill Links Championship along with its neighbors, the Old Course at St. Andrews and Carnoustie. This European Tour event alternates between these three courses. Every hole at Kingsbarns, from the very start, is a new adventure. This is certainly true of the 3rd hole, a par 5 with deep bunkers lying in wait to the right of the green. The 6th hole,

a "small" par 4, also wins plenty of praise thanks to its long, tiered green. This hole was made famous by none other than Michael Phelps (yes, the swimmer), who sank a 52-yard (48 m) putt during a pro-am event in 2012. On the back nine, the 12th (a par 3) and 15th (a par 5) will live on forever in the minds of the lucky players who take on these holes perched on the edge of the ragged coastline — especially the 15th, which is bordered by trees and sea along its entire length to a green fully encircled by water. Some like to compare it to the legendary 18th hole at California's Pebble Beach — high praise indeed!

"Pulling a Van de Velde" has now become a common expression among golfers. It means losing a round in improbable fashion despite having a comfortable lead. In July 1999, on the par-4 18th hole of the championship course, the Frenchman Jean Van de Velde managed to achieve this unlikely feat while on the verge of winning the British Open. With just one hole to play, he had a cushion of three shots on his rivals. Did what happened next come down to an excess of optimism? A moment of madness? A lack of experience? Van de Velde went on to make a bad situation worse, making some terrible decisions that left him deep in the rough off the fairway, under water in a brook and plugged into a sandy bunker. He ended up making a triple bogey, forcing him into a playoff. Mentally exhausted, he faded, handing the victory to Paul Lawrie. And with that, Van de Velde left an indelible mark on history, undoubtedly more so than if he had gone on to win the British Open.

Established
1842

Par
72

Length
6,941 yards
(6,347 m)

Green fees*
US $21–127
*Additional fees subject to change.

Carnoustie Golf Links *Carnoustie, Scotland*

Some call it "The Beast." Others have nicknamed it "Car-nasty." Psychologists use the expression "the Carnoustie effect" to describe a deep feeling of disillusionment. Welcome to Carnoustie Golf Links, the host of eight British Opens and where golf has been played for over four centuries. The stream running through its 18th hole, thought by many to be the hardest final hole on the planet, has claimed countless victims and lost balls. However, the same could also be said of the other 17 holes, with their aggressive fairways, gusty winds coming in from the North Sea and plethora of cavernous bunkers. The 17th hole (above) is the jewel in the crown of a series of three holes widely considered to be the hardest in the world. There is also the legendary 519-yard (475 m) par-5 6th, renamed "Hogan's Alley" in 2003 in memory of the American champion who won here in 1953, known for his cool head and the quality of his swing. "This course is hard but fair. It's the ultimate test," said Tiger Woods, who knows what he is talking about, having never won here. While the championship course might strike fear into players' hearts, there are two other more manageable courses: the Carnoustie Buddon, dating from 1981, and the Burnside. The challenge of the latter is surviving holes 5 and 14 and the combination of the 17th and 18th holes! At Carnoustie, it's never over until it's over.

The long beach of Cruden Bay is known for its pretty pink sand. It was also made famous by Norwegian Tryggve Gran, who became the first person to fly over the North Sea, in 1914. In 1899, the dunes surrounding it enabled Old Tom Morris and Archie Simpson to design a course of isolated holes to give players a unique feeling of seclusion. A new course with a few minor changes made by Tom Simpson and Herbert Fowler emerged in 1926. At the time, the railway company that owned the land wanted to create an upscale vacation venue for London's upper crust. Although the golf course survived, the same cannot be said for the luxurious pink granite hotel, the Palace in the Sandhills, which was demolished in the economic crisis of the 1950s and replaced by a more modern clubhouse. From the course, you can make out the ruins of a very special building, just behind Port Erroll. Stain Castle was said to have inspired *Dracula* novelist Bram Stoker.

Established
1899

Par
70

Length
6,609 yards
(6,043 m)

Green fees*
US $102–174
*Additional fees subject to change.

Cruden Bay Golf Club   *Cruden Bay, Scotland*

If you ever have the chance to tour Scotland's many famous golf courses, be sure to visit Cruden Bay Golf Club and its championship course, especially if you love links courses. Admittedly less prestigious than St. Andrews and Carnoustie, this course is outstanding nonetheless. Its features make it a unique experience. Quite hilly and with imposing dunes, this 6,560-yard (6,000 m) long championship course offers a dazzling variety of holes. While some are more traditional, others are decidedly eccentric or unusual. For instance, on this course, the speed of the greens varies from hole to hole. This is what gives Cruden Bay its charm, but it is also a course that allows you to score well, providing you catch it on a good day, without too much wind. The highlights of the course include the par-4 4th, which offers two great views. To the left is the village and its rooftops, and to the right is the North Sea and its oil tankers. No player can recover if they veer off to the left on the 9th hole, which runs alongside the beach below and whose tiered green offers a panoramic view of the surroundings. The 14th is decent too. It's a compact par 4 with a bathtub-shaped steep-sided green that is well worth a look. And though it may look like a bathtub, there are no water obstacles in sight.

While it is agreed that modern golf was created in Scotland, it is hard to say whether Aberdeen, St. Andrews or Edinburgh has the best claim to be its birthplace. In any case, it is on the Queen's Links, the former site of the Royal Aberdeen, where history records the very first hole, dating back to 1625. Founded in 1780, the club invested the Balgownie links a good century later, before Edward VII granted it its royal distinction. To liven up the game a little, members decided to limit the time spent looking for lost balls to five minutes. Today, this rule has been reduced to just three minutes! The world's sixth oldest golf course was designed by the Simpson brothers, Archie (who also worked on Cruden Bay and Nairn) and Robert (the co-designer of Carnoustie), and it was later remodeled by James Braid, creating the layout it has today. There are several links courses around Aberdeen, and they are all quite different. You can continue your golfing tour by following the coast up to Cruden Bay.

Established
1780

Par
71

Length
6,884 yards
(6,295 m)

Green fees*
US $116–330

*Additional fees subject to change.

Royal Aberdeen Golf Club   *Aberdeen, Scotland*

Whenever you think about British links courses, the Royal Aberdeen Golf Club and its Balgownie Course quickly come to mind. Along Scotland's magnificent and wild east coast, under ever-changing skies, this course is one of the best examples of an intertwining of nature and golf. For plenty of players, the first half of Aberdeen, which runs along the coast, is among the best front nines in the world. The first hole, for instance, is whipped by an easterly wind and faces the sea, which is almost always scattered with supertankers. Here, the grass in the rough scratches at your knees, the fairways are extremely bumpy and most of the greens are heavily protected. The par-3 8th offers highly variable conditions (a 3-iron

might be needed one day, while a pitching wedge is required the next) and has become the course's iconic hole. Ten dragon-toothed bunkers surround the green, and the only way to get near the flag is to stay toward the center and go straight down its throat, according to the local expression. And with high-level courses come international competitions. Among others, the Royal Aberdeen has hosted the Senior British Open (2005), the Walker Cup (2011), the amateur Ryder Cup and the Scottish Open (2014).

Two years after opening, Castle Stuart had already become a venue on the pro circuit. In 2011, the course hosted the Scottish Open for the first time. This was noteworthy because this European Tour event had been held at the same course, Loch Lomond, about 20 miles (32 km) northwest of Glasgow, for the past 15 years. The event's promoters, however, might have felt cursed for having made the change. The first time the event was held at Castle Stuart was a complete disaster due to a huge summer storm, which forced the organizers to reduce the tournament to just 54 holes. The Englishman Luke Donald, number one in the world at the time, emerged from the deluge, winning the title four shots ahead of the field. Fortunately, these exploits didn't dampen the organizers' enthusiasm, and the Scottish Open returned to Castle Stuart in 2012 (won by Jeev Milkha Singh), 2013 (won by Phil Mickelson) and again in 2016 (won by Alex Noren).

Established
2009

Par
72

Length
7,009 yards
(6,409 m)

Green fees*
US $97–277
*Additional fees subject to change.

Castle Stuart Golf Links *Inverness, Scotland*

Like its distant cousin Kingsbarns, Castle Stuart was a success as soon as it opened in 2009. With the breathtaking panorama of the south bank of the Moray Firth, the large inlet in the north of Scotland, this course is also the work of American Mark Parsinen. Just like Kingsbarns, it is a work of wonder and a world-class golf course. Its designer explains that the layout is based on a philosophy of the "recoverable error." In other words, everyone plays bad shots, including the pros, and the most interesting aspect of golf is a player's ability to recover from them. Consequently, Castle Stuart's wide fairways are bounded by gorse, broom, heather and beach grass. The greens are undulating but not excessively so. The course is spectacular from the very start, with the first three holes running along the seafront. It then heads inland, and the holes become more undulating. If you had to pick one hole to highlight in particular (which is not easy here!), it would probably be the 551-yard (504 m) par-5 6th, which ends with a narrow green protected on either side by two very wide bunkers. On the back nine, the 220-yard (201 m) 17th hole on the cliff top provides an intimidating challenge. At Castle Stuart, thrills are guaranteed.

Every family needs an eccentric who stands out from the rest. When it comes to golf, it has to be Shiskine! What makes Shiskine so unique? First of all, this course only has 12 holes! The First World War left six of its holes in a terrible state, and they were never restored. Moreover, the club, founded in 1895, advocates a traditional, old-school style of golf. It might make today's course designers smile, but it proves that you can create enjoyment without the need for time-consuming and expensive work to construct greens. The course was designed by Willie Fernie, a professional player and architect born in St. Andrews who remodeled the Old Course, among others. On the Isle of Arran, Shiskine's old-world charm attracts players just as much as the magnificent scenery of the Kilbrannan Sound. Paul McCartney immortalized the nearby Mull of Kinture, where he used to own a home, in a song of the same name.

Established
1895

Par
42

Length
2,995 yards
(2,739 m)

Green fees*
US $26–56
*Additional fees subject to change.

Shiskine Golf and Tennis Club *Isle of Arran, Scotland*

You need to have your wits about you at Shiskine. Almost every hole has a hidden section, either from the tee or on the approach to the flag. This tortuously twisting, chaotic course represents a huge challenge for any golfer. The layout is so unusual and curious that signposts have been installed at certain places to ensure players keep going in the right direction. Seven of the 12 holes around this coastal course are par-3s, but which hole does everyone talk about? The par-3 3rd hole, known as the "Crow's Nest." The green, completely hidden from the tee, is situated high above on a tier protected by brush. You can sometimes see a flag, which appears to mark the hole... but no! It is actually there to tell the next player that the green is free and that they can safely play their shot. To reach the green after your tee shot, you need to climb a small staircase, offering a moment of suspense while you wait to see whether your ball has landed near the hole... or has been lost for good. Although Shiskine is a quick course (2 hours and 15 minutes on average), it is so enjoyable that people often play it twice.

The history of Turnberry is yet another example of the link between the origins of golf and the development of rail travel. With the opening of a new rail line, the Marquess of Ailsa came up with the idea of building a course at Turnberry on land that wasn't suitable for farming. Turnberry was an instant success and was soon hosting its first professional tournament. During the two World Wars, the course was transformed into a military base, with the fairways flattened to allow planes to land and the hotel converted into a field hospital. There is a memorial commemorating this period near the 9th hole. Kintyre, the second course, has kept the same layout but was significantly modified by Martin Ebert. Several new bunkers were created along with a water hazard between holes 5 and 13. The direction of play was reversed on several holes, increasing the difficulty level and offering unobstructed views of the lighthouse and the ruins of Robert the Bruce's castle.

Established
1902

Par
71

Length
6,473 yards
(5,919 m)

Green fees*
US $214–698
*Additional fees subject to change.

Turnberry Golf Club *Turnberry, Scotland*

When a course has hosted the British Open on four separate occasions, you know you are dealing with something special. Top of the class in every way, Turnberry offers spectacular views of the Firth of Clyde, the Mull of Kintyre and the Isle of Arran and iconic holes like the famous 9th (above) on the magical Ailsa Course, with a lighthouse overlooking the green. Everything comes together here for a unique golfing experience. Designed by Philip Mackenzie Ross and modernized by Martin Ebert, Ailsa is a high-level course that, after the 3rd hole, leaves no room for error. With raised greens, devilishly positioned bunkers and imposing dunes, especially along holes 4 to 11, the course's eight coastal holes often take the

brunt of the wind. It is also something very special to walk the course that went down in sports history thanks to the famous duel between Americans Jack Nicklaus and Tom Watson during the 1977 Open. Watson claimed the famous winner's Claret Jug by finishing one shot ahead despite an incredible final putt by his rival. In tribute to that epic battle and the wonderful weather that day, the 18th hole on the Ailsa Course was nicknamed the "Duel in the Sun." Bragging about the sunshine in Scotland suggests more than a hint of British humor!

Portrush or Royal County Down? This is the dilemma faced by golfers doing a tour of Northern Irish golf courses. The first offers an almost perfect layout, with undulating fairways and plenty of doglegs. The second provides breathtaking views, eccentricity and blind shots on narrower and more demanding fairways. In short, there is very little to choose between them. In any case, the Royal County Down has been used as a template by the new generation of golf course architects, who take inspiration from these traditional links to come up with new courses of the same standard. However, sites like the Murlough Nature Reserve in the Dundrum Bay, with the Mourne Mountains in the background, have become exceedingly rare! Royal County Down is so successful today thanks to the great many talents that contributed to its creation. The first on that list is Old Tom Morris, the grandfather of golf, who designed the course. Although it has been significantly remodeled over time, it has remained true to its origins.

Established
1889

Par
71

Length
7,160 yards
(6,547 m)

Green fees*
US $135–154
*Additional fees subject to change.

Royal County Down Golf Club *Newcastle, Northern Ireland*

When you ask experienced golfers who have traveled widely where they would like to play their final round, Royal County Down Golf Club comes very high up on the list. On the east coast of Northern Ireland opposite the Isle of Man, the club is in a breathtaking location with a view over dunes as far as the eye can see. Thanks to the cleverly varied orientation of the holes on the flagship course, the Championship Links, players can enjoy the surroundings to their fullest. The excellence also extends to the golf itself, with a varied terrain that features harmonious, quick and occasionally domed greens and plenty of blind shots too. The bunkers are sometimes referred to as having "beards" due to the world-famous tall grasses

encircling them. And then there's the famous 9th hole. This 486-yard (444 m) par 4 is one of the most photographed holes in the world, a real roller-coaster ride with a maximum elevation change of a good 66 feet (20 m). Players are well advised to hit a very good second shot or risk having to deal with the first two bunkers surrounding the green. The Royal County also has a second course, the Annesley Links, which is a little shorter than its big brother but gives less advanced players the chance to fully enjoy the Royal County experience.

To the immense pride of the Royal Portrush Golf Club, the Dunluce Links is the only course not on the island of Great Britain to have hosted the British Open. It was first held here in 1951 and then again in 2019, after a long break due to the decades of political turbulence that shook Ireland. But the RPGC is now back among the 15 or so links courses that host this sports showpiece. To celebrate its return in 2019, the Dunluce Links got a makeover for the first time since 1932, when it was redesigned by Harry Colt. This time, the task was entrusted to Martin Ebert,

who changed the layout of holes 17 and 18 and created two new holes (the 7th and 8th) using part of the land from the Valley Course. The return of Portrush to the British Open family saw a win for Irishman Shane Lowry, who finished ahead of Englishman Tommy Fleetwood. The RPGC is scheduled to host two more British Opens by 2040.

Established
1888

Par
72

Length
7,316 yards
(6,690 m)

Green fees*
US $110–295

*Additional fees subject to change.

Royal Portrush Golf Club *Portrush, Northern Ireland*

At the great banquet table of golf that is available across the British Isles, Northern Ireland will not be outdone. In fact, the Royal Portrush Golf Course, located on Northern Ireland's north coast, is among the most popular. The Valley Links and, in particular, the Dunluce Links have gained worldwide fame after hosting the British Open. The course takes its name from the ruins of a castle that are visible from the green of the 5th hole. Portrush, a links with typically British characteristics, is a very high level course with narrow fairways, dense roughs that players are well advised to steer clear of and numerous fiendishly positioned bunkers. Among various wonders, this course has two holes that make players' mouths water the

world over. The first is the 382-yard (349 m) par-4 5th, which faces the ocean with a dogleg and a raised tee. A slightly overzealous approach will leave you in the sand of White Rocks beach just below the green. Then, on the back nine, comes Calamity Corner (the 16th hole), a 235-yard (215 m) par 3 that is iconic in the world of golf. There is a chasm between the tee and the green that you must avoid at all costs. With such a breathtaking view and the imperative to hit a great shot, the hardest thing on this hole is keeping a cool head.

At Lahinch, one could easily conclude that the goats predict the weather. The animal has been featured on the club's official badge since the 1950s because players noticed that the goats grazing on the course tended to approach the clubhouse when it was about to rain, meaning that it was time to get your rain gear out. After opening in 1892, Lahinch very quickly established high standards, earning the nickname "the Irish St. Andrews." The Old Course has never stopped evolving over time, constantly improving without losing its natural assets, thanks to the biggest names in course architecture and design: Old Tom Morris (1892), Alister MacKenzie (1927) and Martin Hawtree (1999), whose revisions brought the course closer to the dunes. The ruins of Dough Castle provide a magnificent backdrop to the 7th hole with a wonderful view of the Atlantic to boot. The single wall left standing is all that remains of this castle built back in the 14th century, but there are rumors that its ghosts still haunt the dunes.

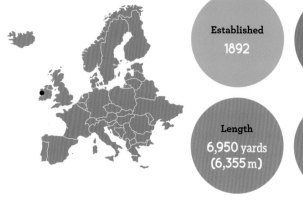

Established
1892

Par
72

Length
6,950 yards
(6,355 m)

Green fees*
US $150–258
*Additional fees subject to change.

Lahinch Golf Club *Lahinch, Ireland*

In the big and beautiful family of British-style links courses, Lahinch, on the east coast of Ireland, in the north of the province of Munster, is undoubtedly among the most spectacular. Its character is born from an extremely successful combination of the natural surroundings and its two traditional courses packed with history. The holes on the club's most prestigious layout, the Old Course, wind their way between the dunes, some of which are the size of imposing hills, half facing the ocean and the other half turned toward the village. It is hard to pick one hole that stands out above the rest — you could choose seven or eight — because the course is such a consistent, high-quality and strategic blend of

short and long holes, blind greens and doglegs. This variety is clear from the range of both broad and narrow fairways, roughs of varying density depending on the hole and the position of the bunkers. Its fine layout even attracted the professional circuit, which picked it as an event venue. The Old Course hosted the Irish Open, an event on the European Tour, for the first time in 2019. There can be little doubt that this event will return soon, just as it is difficult to imagine playing golf in Ireland without stopping off at Lahinch.

Lahinch Golf Club *Lahinch, Ireland*

After walking part of the bare coastline on which he would go on to create the course, Arnold Palmer said that he had "never come across a piece of land so ideally suited for the building of a golf course." Tralee Golf Club has existed since 1896, but back then it was split between a first nine holes at Mounthawk and a second nine in Fenit. The location of Barrow Point was a good compromise for everyone, and Palmer designed his first European course there in 1984. The towering US champion, ever the charismatic figure, helped to popularize his sport when golf competitions started to be shown on television. Nicknamed "The King," he rivaled Jack Nicklaus as both a player and a course architect. At Tralee, Palmer wanted a highly varied course that stimulated the senses without diminishing any of the incredible panoramic scene. The beach below the course was the location for the filming of *Ryan's Daughter*. The David Lean movie went on to give its name to the 17th hole (above).

Established
1896

Par
72

Length
6,990 yards
(6,392 m)

Green fees*
US $268
*Additional fees subject to change.

Tralee Golf Club *Ardfert, Ireland*

Anyone on a golfing trip to the British Isles cannot afford to miss Tralee Golf Club. Sometimes underestimated, this links course offers very different front and back nines, which makes it such an interesting course. But rest assured that the panorama on offer is wonderful from any perspective. The first section, close to the Atlantic Ocean, is very flat and gives players a good chance to find their feet, especially since getting used to the wind is essential. According to top players, the second half is tougher. Dotted with huge dunes, the course becomes more undulating. Some even compare it to Ballybunion. The most popular hole is the par-3 16th, which has a raised tee and waves lapping at the green, which is

heavily protected by three bunkers. In the background, on the other side of the bay, stand the often snow-capped summits of the Dingle Peninsula. It's magical! You need a good drive to get over a small, steep-sided gully, and the rough here is particularly inhospitable. There must be quite an assortment of lost balls hiding in the long grass. Fortunately, the very flat green is not too much of a challenge. This hole is the epitome of the two sides of Tralee: challenge and enjoyment.

Picture the scene: Tom Simpson, as famous for his courses as he is for his eccentricity, arrives at Ballybunion in his chauffeur-driven Rolls Royce with the golfing champion Molly Gourlay on his arm. They picnic on the course to immerse themselves in its surroundings and consider what changes need to be made. Simpson had the good sense to understand that nature made this links course what it was and that any changes needed to be made with surgical precision. The other Tom to whom Ballybunion owes a great deal is Tom Watson. Golf's

emblematic figure of the 70s and 80s raised the profile of the Old Course, especially among American golfers, who enjoy English and Scottish links courses: "Nobody can call themselves a golfer until they have played at Ballybunion," he said. "You would think the game originated there." Despite its remoteness, Ballybunion saw a stratospheric rise in its reputation. The Cashen Course, opened in 1982, benefits from an equally outstanding location. It is a roller-coaster ride of a course, as charming as it is surprising.

Established
1893

Par
71

Length
6,801 yards
(6,219 m)

Green fees*
US $268
*Additional fees subject to change.

Ballybunion Golf Club *Ballybunion, Ireland*

Of the links most likely to separate the most talented players from the rest, the Old Course at Ballybunion on the west coast of Ireland is near the top of the list. Players who reach the clubhouse after playing to their handicap (or even beating it) traditionally celebrate with a good single malt. None other than Bill Clinton visited here in September 1998, during his second term in office. Despite a perhaps overzealous use of the mulligan, he loved the course so much that he came back in 2001, after leaving the White House. In the village of Ballybunion stands a statue of the man himself, club in hand, commemorating the presidential visit. With the wind an almost constant fixture, it is tough to finish your round unscathed, but the Old Course nevertheless remains a genuine pleasure for anyone who visits it. Despite its impressive start running alongside a cemetery, this course is less spectacular during its opening six inland holes. It really comes into its own on the coastal holes 7 to 17. The Old Course is particularly known for the quality of its par 3s. For instance, the brilliant sequence of holes 14 and 15 starts with an ultra-compact par 3 followed by another much longer one heading toward the beach. It is impossible to pick one or two standout holes, some tentatively suggest the 11th (above), which underlines the consistency of the course as a whole — a sign of real quality.

Ballybunion Golf Club *Ballybunion, Ireland*

The Old Head of Kinsale is the flight of fancy of Irish businessman John O'Connor, who bought the rocky outcrop with his brother in 1989 with the aim of making it into one of the world's top-ten golf courses, perhaps maybe even the best. Although it prides itself on having hosted Tiger Woods and Bill Clinton, it has alienated environmentalists, ornithologists and hikers, whose legal action was eventually dismissed by the courts. It certainly is a historic place, having previously been highly prized by the Vikings and then the Celts and Normans. The Stone of Accord (featured on the club's logo) was still used at the start of the century to conclude important agreements, by shaking hands through its hole. Old Head is also known for the many shipwrecks that occurred here, hence the lighthouse, a modern version of the primitive signals that shone unceasingly down through the centuries. Other than playing golf, and subject to prior consent, you can gain access to the cliffs for fishing, birdwatching or even spotting whales as they pass by the shore.

Established
1997

Par
72

Length
7,100 yards
(6,492 m)

Green fees*
US $215

*Additional fees subject to change.

Old Head Golf Links   *Kinsale, Ireland*

Golfers who visit Old Head describe it as an unforgettable, one-of-a-kind experience. While this course is almost certainly not the best in this book, it is arguably the most original, wildest and most spectacular. It is located on a 220-acre (89 ha) peninsula, whose cliffs stretch almost 2 miles (3 km) into the Atlantic Ocean! The setting and views are breathtaking, making you wish you were a bird so that you could enjoy them to their fullest. There are thrills aplenty, especially around the nine cliff-top holes with waves crashing 300 feet (90 m) below. Be warned: only a thin rope separates players from the abyss, and the wind, as you would expect, never takes a day off. Indeed, the unrelenting gusts make it impossible for any trees to grow here. Old Head is not just a series of holes in an outstanding setting. The weather conditions alone would make it a very high-level course, despite having multiple tees. Experts consider the par 3s, such as holes 7, 13 and 16, to be exceptional. The highlight is undoubtedly the 622-yard (569 m) par-5 17th hole with the ocean on the right and the iconic black-and-white lighthouse dead ahead. Splendid! The hardest thing about Old Head? Trying not to get your camera out every few minutes!

As is often the case, the clubhouse separates the two courses at St. Enodoc. The Holywell Course, shorter and less undulating than its big brother, was originally made up of nine holes and was completely remodeled in 1982, when the club bought more land. In total, there are now nine par 3s and nine par 4s. Holywell is so named because of the supposedly sacred well by hole 12. Legend has it that the inhabitants of St. Enodoc came here to baptize the converted. Nowadays, it mostly attracts converts to golf! Like Augusta, the Holywell Course has its own "Amen Corner," but on an obviously smaller scale. The series of holes 14, 15 and 16 is fiendishly challenging, with the highlight of the three perhaps being the 14th. With a dogleg to the right and a raised green, players need to advance without a view of the flag for a large part of the hole. Holywell is admittedly a relatively high-level course, but it is also recommended for those looking to improve their skills.

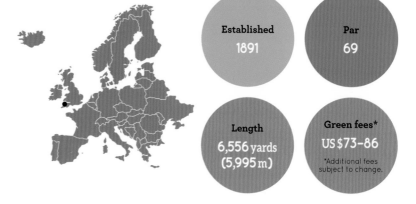

Established
1891

Par
69

Length
6,556 yards
(5,995 m)

Green fees*
US $73-86
*Additional fees subject to change.

St. Enodoc Golf Club *Rock, England*

A coastal resort nicknamed "England's Saint-Tropez," the fishermen's village of Rock, Cornwall, is most well-known for its watersports. Nonetheless, with its two splendid links courses, Church Course and Hollywell Course, overlooking the estuary, golf has also been a major feature in the area since 1891. These two relatively hilly courses are set among imposing sand dunes covered in wild, fragrant sea grass. Designed by James Braid, Church Course owes its name to the 11th-century church located to the right of the 10th green. This 456-yard (417 m) par 4 is unarguably the course's flagship hole. It is so devilishly difficult that some play it as a par 5, with a water hazard, consistently narrow fairway and dogleg finish that turns sharply to the left. Once you get near the flag, putting next to a church is a special experience. Players also come to St. Enodoc to take on the challenge of hole 6 and its incredible (and completely unique) Himalaya Bunker (next spread). This incredibly vast expanse of sand is dug into the side of a hill to the right of the green, which reaches a height of around 75 feet (23 m) at its summit! Unless you are an expert at getting out of bunkers, you might find yourself having to play backward on this topsy-turvy hole before aiming for the green!

St. Enodoc Golf Club *Rock, England*

In a country renowned for its links, Sunningdale can legitimately make a claim to be one of the best inland courses. Developed on land owned by St. John's College, Cambridge, each hole was designed to be in harmony with nature. It was somewhat of a revolution when it was established, since some said that it was impossible to create perfect greens so far from the sea. The other challenge was working out how to get golfers there, since cars were still very much in their infancy. Sunningdale became just a train ride away from London thanks to a timely offer of a membership card to the director of railways. Since then, the Old Course has hosted many prestigious national and international competitions. Despite being considered one of the most beautiful golf courses in Britain, it will never host the British Open because Sunningdale is not a links course, unlike Royal St. George's Golf Club (next spread), which has hosted it 14 times.

Established
1901

Par
70

Length
6,729 yards
(6,153 m)

Green fees*
US $337
*Additional fees subject to change.

Sunningdale Golf Club *Sunningdale, England*

People don't come to Sunningdale to play 18 holes, but 36. With two outstanding and challenging courses, it is considered one of the United Kingdom's must-play golfing venues. In the middle of the 1920s, the club decided to create a second course to meet growing demand, and so the New Course was built to accompany the already renowned Old Course. It was the handiwork of course architect Harry Colt, who had already made some changes to the original course. The New Course is more open than its older brother, with fewer trees obstructing play. It still presents a stern test with plenty of doglegs, raised tees, consistent undulation and narrow fairways. The Old Course, designed by double British championship winner Willie Park Junior, opened in 1901. The Scottish champion was renowned for the quality of his putting. As a result, he paid particular attention to the greens on this woodland course, which are both wide and set on the natural topography of the site. The Old Course (above) is also known for the length and density of the heather surrounding it. Legendary golf courses have no shortage of iconic holes. After playing the Old Course, the visual wonders of the 399-yard (365 m) par-4 5th and 467-yard (427 m) par-4 10th live long in the memory.

Royal St. George's Golf Club *Kent, England*

At the start of the last century, Étretat was mainly visited by vacationing Parisians, but plenty of UK tourists also traveled here, and they were quick to seek out their favorite leisure activities. As a result, the lawn tennis club was founded in 1908, along with a golf course overlooking the chalk cliffs, between two emblematic locations: the Pointe de la Courtine and the Porte d'Aval. It even had an impressive clubhouse on what is now the 11th hole, where you could have a cup of tea before going pigeon shooting near the Manneporte. The leading light in French golf, Arnaud Massy, designed the course with architect Julien Chantepie. Initially an 11-hole course, it was expanded to 18 holes after the First World War before being ravaged by fighting during the Second World War. Extensively modified in 1992, it now covers some 4 miles (6 km) along the Custom Officer's path (*Sentier des Douaniers*), which is especially busy in the summer months. At Étretat, there is always an audience, putting a little bit of extra pressure on players' shoulders.

Established	Par
1908	72

Length	Green fees*
6,577 yards (6,014 m)	US $60–83 *Additional fees subject to change.

Golf d'Étretat   *Upper Normandy, Étretat, France*

With an exceptional setting, high-quality layout and magnificent light, Étretat is without a doubt one of France's most otherworldly coastal golf courses. Of the 18 holes, five of them (4, 10, 12, 13 and 14) face the sea, almost on the edge of the cliffs, more than 300 feet (100 m) above the waves. Players come to Étretat to post a decent score, but it is very rare for them to overcome the urge to get their phone out to capture the moment as the wonder of the setting overcomes their concentration. And you need plenty of focus on the course's flagship 446-yard (408 m) par-5 10th hole — an impressive and complex challenge with raised tees and a very slightly S-shaped layout. Its off-camber fairway has the bad habit of sending

balls bouncing into the rough. The green is protected by three bunkers, and with a course boundary on the right, this hole is enough to drive you mad. In a previous event, one unfortunate (but admittedly persistent) player took 33 shots to finish the hole. The 4th could also make a claim to be the course's signature hole, with its green overlooking the English Channel, giving you the feeling that you are playing among the waves from your second shot, especially since this is where you can really start to feel the wind blow — a permanent fixture of golf in Normandy. Étretat is also well-known for its warm welcome and friendliness. The clubhouse is the best place to finish off a nice day of golf.

The 2018 Ryder Cup held at Golf National put France back on the golfing map and marked only the second time in the history of the event, founded in 1927, that it was hosted outside the United States or United Kingdom. Only Valderrama, Spain, shares this privilege, having hosted in 1997. Every two years, the Ryder Cup pits the United States against Europe in a team battle with a match-play format involving both singles and doubles play. The Ryder Cup, which attracts a billion passionate TV viewers around the world, is the third most widely covered sporting event after the FIFA World Cup and the Olympic Games. The event in France attracted 270,000 spectators in three days. They witnessed a victory for the Europeans despite the much anticipated return of Tiger Woods to Team USA. This also confirmed the Old Continent's domination, the team having won nine of the last twelve Ryder Cup matches.

Established
1990

Par
72

Length
7,330 yards
(6,703 m)

Green fees*
US $96–155
*Additional fees
subject to change.

Le Golf National *Saint-Quentin-en-Yvelines, Île-de-France, France*

Since 1990, the little white ball has had a home of its very own in France: Golf National, 40 minutes southwest of Paris. Commissioned by the French Golf Federation, the site has three courses: the Albatros caters to high level players, the Aigle (French for "eagle") is open to all and the Oiselet (or "chick") is, a nine-hole training course. Designed by architect Hubert Chesneau, a former top-level player and director of the French Golf Federation, in collaboration with Robert Von Hagge, these three courses were founded on an original philosophy. "My aim," explained the creator, "was to build a stadium for golf that could host major events. Unlike a lot of courses built on natural, relatively undulating ground, I wanted to shape the topography as well as design the course itself in order to create natural spectator seating." The Albatros course that emerged as a result is generally accepted to be among the best and most striking courses in Europe. A venue for the French Open, an official tournament on the European Tour, and the 2018 Ryder Cup, this par 72 is especially known for its rolling greens, vast, undulating fairways and, above all, last four holes, which are surrounded by water, and have seen plenty of players' dreams sink without a trace. According to Nick Faldo, the first player to win here, in 1991, the Albatros is "tough but fair."

Le Golf National *Saint-Quentin-en-Yvelines, Île-de-France, France*

Most well-known French golf courses are built on amazing family estates or are the result of influential men giving free rein to their passion for the sport. This is certainly the case with Chantilly, where, over 100 years ago, Baron Édouard de Rothschild helped to significantly boost the club's reputation by establishing a second course on the site. The club was then devastated by the Second World War, the courses becoming minefields and the clubhouse partially destroyed. Once restored, Chantilly reestablished its cozy atmosphere, and the return of its enormous clock preserved its Sunningdale-esque ambiance, which adds to the distinctly British feel of the place. The fingerprints of Tom Simpson are evident on the course, with merciless bunkers and holes as varied as they are challenging from start to finish, though the back nine is generally considered better. Above all, though, despite being on the outskirts of Paris, the feeling of being completely cut off from the rest of the world is why golfers love Chantilly so much.

Established
1909

Par
71

Length
6,998 yards
(6,399 m)

Green fees*
From US $53
*Additional fees subject to change.

Golf de Chantilly   *Vineuil-Saint-Firmin, Hauts-de-France, France*

A clear idea of tradition, two courses packed full of history and a prestigious setting... You would be forgiven for thinking you were on the other side of the English Channel, but you just need to drive an hour north of Paris to end up in this golfing paradise. Vineuil is very much an old-school course. It has hosted the French Open on multiple occasions, with Nick Faldo winning back-to-back titles here in 1988 and 1989. The Englishman arrived that year having just won the first of his three Masters titles. At Vineuil, you need more than just long drives to post a decent score. You also need plenty of accuracy to avoid ending up among the trees bordering the narrow fairways and, needless to say, the hundred or so devilishly positioned bunkers. The second course at Chantilly, Les Longères, has a colorful history. Reduced to nine holes after the Second World War, it was returned to its original length in the late 1980s, thanks in particular to the work of course architect Donald Steel. Less popular than Vineuil, Les Longères nonetheless tends to be pretty high up in the rankings. Much more than a last resort, it enables visitors to enjoy timeless moments in an exceptional setting. After all, isn't that exactly why so many come to play at clubs of Chantilly's caliber?

Golf in the Île-de-France region owes a great deal to Tom Simpson, the great course architect of the first half of the 20th century, who redesigned Fontainebleau in 1920, after reworking courses at Morfontaine and Chantilly. Originally designed by Julien Chantepie, Fontainebleau is one of the oldest courses in France. Remodeled by the Hawke father and son team in the 1960s and again in the 1980s, the course had its defenses significantly strengthened while maintaining the Simpson touch with over 100 bunkers. The layout of some holes is reminiscent of some top UK courses much loved by players. Often reducing the rough to a small strip, the dense forest can be particularly unforgiving to players having a bad day, especially from the back tees. But that is part of Fontainebleau's charm. The advantage of the sandy soil is that you can play here regardless of the weather conditions. And since the future of golf and the planet are intertwined, 30 or so sheep have been tasked with maintaining the course between holes 4 and 5.

Established
1909

Par
72

Length
6,579 yards
(6,016 m)

Green fees*
US $85–108
*Additional fees subject to change.

Golf de Fontainebleau *Fontainebleau, Île-de-France, France*

Although its ranking can vary, the course at Fontainebleau has long been among the best-rated golfing venues in Europe. This course is not hugely long, but its small greens, narrow fairways, hellish bunkers and environment make it a stern test for any golfer. A royal hunting ground in times gone by, playing in this beech, oak and pine forest lush with heather and broom is widely considered a must. The edges of the course are dotted with a number of boulders typical of Fontainebleau, thus giving this 6,579-yard (6,016 m) course its own unique identity. The most famous holes here are the 12th and 15th. The 12th, a par 5 at 455 yards (416 m), can turn into a nightmare if you fail to avoid the innumerable bunkers on the

fairway and the large rocky area just at the foot of the green. And just when you think you're out of the woods, you have to deal with a highly unpredictable green. The 15th, a par 4 at 453 yards (414 m), is a blind hole where you need to drive over the top of the heather or rough. Reminiscent of the 15th hole at Cruden Bay, the difficulty of this hole is the subject of a great many conversations and debates. But the beauty of golf is being able to relive the round again once you are safely in the clubhouse, especially one as charming as Fontainebleau.

Morfontaine is a strictly private affair! From the six holes created on a polo pitch by the Gramont family to the Grand Parcours, where only the lucky few get to play. While the Duke of Guiche wanted to expand access to the club, asking Tom Simpson to create a second course in 1927, he certainly wasn't intending to let the general public in. If you'd like to access the very exclusive Morfontaine, you're best bet is to make friends in high places. President Eisenhower was a frequent visitor, and François Mitterrand used to play on Tuesdays, when the club was closed. They enjoyed the solitude and calmness of the course, its huge trees and its perfect upkeep but also the old-world charm of the red brick clubhouse, where time seems to have stood still. After the Grand Parcours, anyone spending the day at Morfontaine mustn't forget to head straight to Vallière, the original nine-hole course with outstanding greens, to make your timeless trip last a little bit longer.

Established
1927

Par
70

Length
6,563 yards
(6,001m)

Green fees
Invitation only

Golf de Morfontaine   *Morfontaine, Picardie, France*

If you want a happy life, stay well hidden! That could be the motto of this legendary private club. Thankfully, a lucky few have had access to this temple of golf and can attest to the course's excellence. This French-style Augusta is considered to be one of the most stunning courses in Europe, perhaps the world. Like the Masters course, it is first and foremost the enchanting greenery that stands out at this site covering 383 acres (155 ha). Centuries-old pines, heather, broom, birch and oaks stand beside huge boulders (including one in the shape of a frog alongside hole 14). They provide a stunning and wonderfully silent backdrop to this course, free from water hazards, where golf carts are strictly forbidden.

When it comes to the golf itself, the legendary architect Tom Simpson riddled the course with challenges before Kyle Phillips made a few more changes. The course is a mix of short and long holes; a series of six consecutive par 4s, from the 5th to the 10th hole (with a dogleg on the 8th); perfectly manicured fairways; and rolling, off-camber greens protected by clutches of bunkers, most of which are naturally positioned. For a little historical context, the Grand Parcours was opened by Simone Thion de La Chaume, who later became Madame Lacoste, the first foreigner to win the British Amateur Championship, in 1924. At Morfontaine, you either go chic or you go home!

Baron Bich, famous for his pens and disposable razors, is responsible for this superb and mysterious course that is hidden amid a wooded estate covering 1,606 acres (650 ha). To create the course of his dreams, Baron Bich gave carte blanche to US architect Robert Von Hagge, who would later go on to design Le Golf National. The result is a very tricky 18 holes. Crazy rumors spread like wildfire around Les Bordes when the estate closed in 2008 after archeological finds were discovered there. Were they going to open to the public? Were they being bought by the Chinese? The business was taken over in 2018 by Driss Benkirane, a golf enthusiast and member of various prestigious clubs around the world. He entrusted the creation of the New Course to Gil Hanse, designer of Castle Stuart and the Olympic course in Rio. The new version of Les Bordes was designed with sustainability in mind. The roughs, which were grown in the UK before being transported to Sologne, are made from fescue, a seed that requires less water and fertilizer.

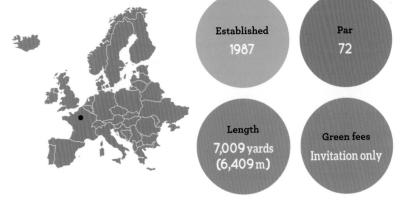

Established
1987

Par
72

Length
7,009 yards
(6,409 m)

Green fees
Invitation only

Les Bordes Golf International   *Saint-Laurent-Nouan, Centre, France*

Every self-respecting golfer dreams of one day playing at Les Bordes. This private club, which attracts people who love golf for golf's sake and a special penchant for secrecy, made that dream even more tantalizing by opening a second course in 2020. Just like a good old UK-style club, you can now choose between the Old Course and the New Course. Both courses offer a comprehensive, high-level golfing experience in the magnificent and peaceful setting of the dense Sologne forest, where you can cross paths with a wandering deer at any moment. They say that most of the holes on the Old Course would be stand-out holes anywhere. Water is the common thread running through this course. There are 12 holes with some kind of water hazard, notably hole 14, where you have to avoid the water twice to land on the green, perched on a peninsula. The layout of the bunkers is remarkable and aggressive, exemplified by the crown of sand encircling the first green. The ocean is far away, but the New Course gets plenty of inspiration from traditional links courses. Indeed, it is notable for the very short distances between the holes, just like the original Scottish courses. Developed on naturally sandy ground, its fairways lined with gorse, broom and heather are also dotted with large, jagged bunkers. The highlight of this course is a 10-foot (3 m) high pot bunker on hole 14. You have been warned!

Walking along the greens amid the fragrances of the neighboring scrubland to reach the magnificent Grand Sperone beach would be enough to make anyone take up golf. This course boasts an outstanding setting overlooking the Mediterranean, with Sardinia and the wild Lavezzi archipelago in the background. The idea of having a golf course in Sperone first emerged in the early 1960s, thanks both to the stunning chalk cliffs nearby and a little bit of luck. Built on a formerly undesirable area of land costing a mere pittance, it has become a popular location for jet-setters. The transformation took 30 years and included the construction of the nearby Figari airport, a long delay due to Corsican nationalists, thwarted extortion attempts and bombing attempts. Eventually, however, these greens towering over the Mediterranean were ready to be played on. According to Robert Trent Jones, the sheer beauty and diversity of holes 12 and 16 make them comparable to the seafront holes at Pebble Beach and Cypress Point. A golf cart is highly recommended on this undulating course in the summer months.

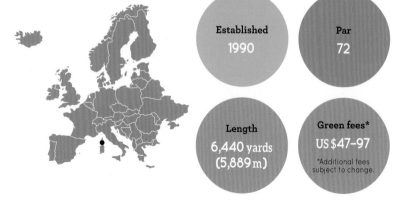

Established
1990

Par
72

Length
6,440 yards
(5,889 m)

Green fees*
US $47–97
*Additional fees subject to change.

Golf de Sperone   *Sperone, Bonifacio, Corsica, France*

An exceptional setting calls for a genius architect. One of the undisputed masters, Robert Trent Jones Senior, creator of almost 500 courses in 35 countries, took on the task of designing what is now considered to be his final masterpiece. The distinctiveness of Sperone lies in its 185 acres (75 ha) of carefully maintained greenery amid a wild setting, with two sets of nine holes that have completely different but complementary features typical of the terrain common to this southernmost tip of Corsica. The difficulty at this inland and highly technical course gradually ramps up during the first half, full of small greens located amid fragrant scrubland. The back nine is more well-known and more spectacular too, as it runs along the open sea. The course at Bonifacio is particularly famous for the sudden gusts that can strike at any moment. Here, wind makes players' lives much more difficult, especially on hole 12, when you have the wind at your back. People also flock to Sperone to try their luck on the course's flagship 16th hole. For the boldest of players looking to reach the green in the shortest possible distance, both the drive from the tee and the second shot on this 470-yard (430 m) cliff-top par 5 need to go over the waves below. There is no room for error. If you lose your ball, it's never coming back!

October 1994, 18th hole, the final day of the Volvo Masters. Severiano Ballesteros is locked in battle with Bernhard Langer to win the title. Suddenly, the ball shoots right on the fairway following his tee shot. The Spaniard's ball ends up at the foot of a tree, gently nestled in a small hole. It was a disaster for Seve, who then tried to curry favor with legendary referee John Paramor. Ballesteros asked for the "burrowing animal" rule to be applied. If a ball falls into a hole made by a rabbit or similar animal, the player is entitled to a free drop without receiving a penalty. The two men consequently launched into a surreal debate about the nature and origin of the hole in question. As much as Paramor tried to find evidence that the hole was made by an animal, like some earth lying next to it, there was nothing to be seen, and he therefore refused to budge. Ballesteros had to chip his ball out to get back on the fairway, which was one shot too many for his championship hopes.

Established
1974

Par
71

Length
6,988 yards
(6,390 m)

Green fees*
US $408
*Additional fees
subject to change.

Real Club Valderrama   *Sotogrande, Spain*

In golf, it's never easy for courses outside the United Kingdom and United States to garner respect and admiration. The Real Club Valderrama is among the few courses to achieve such a feat, under the management of its owner at the time, the late Jaime Ortiz-Patino. Its nickname, the "Augusta of Europe," says a lot about this club's caliber, both behind the scenes and on the very high level course itself, which was designed by American Robert Trent Jones. Among a sea of magnificent (and equally treacherous) cork trees, Valderrama quickly became an essential stop on the international circuit, even becoming the first club in continental Europe to host the Ryder Cup, in 1997. With Seve Ballesteros as captain, the Europeans took the title by one point. There are two holes in particular that golfers the world over dream about. The par-5 4th, which is nicknamed "The Waterfall" after the water hazard situated just behind the green, and the 536-yard (490 m) par-5 17th, with a stream running alongside it and a green protected by a water hazard and two bunkers. This hole became particularly famous when it took center stage for a key moment in the Ryder Cup. It has also been the site of not one but two albatrosses (3 under par), by Miguel Angel Jiménez (1994) and Graeme McDowell (2007). Valderrama is also a wonderful habitat for all kinds of wildlife, including frogs, owls, badgers and butterflies.

The rise of golf in Portugal owes a lot to the English. It all started with the founding of a club to accompany a wine export business in 1890, before Sir Henry Cotton really got things moving in 1966 with Penina, the very first Portuguese golf course. A leading figure in English golf in the 1930s and 1940s, Cotton won the British Open on three occasions in addition to playing in and captaining the European Ryder Cup team. Although Portugal only has 75 clubs, more than half of them are very high-level courses. This is the case for both courses at Vale do Lobo, which offers a mix of links and woodland courses. While the Royal course occasionally flirts with the edge of the high cliffs, the Ocean course provides a more gentle descent to the beach with bumpy fairways lined by pines and eucalyptus trees. It requires accuracy, but in return it offers unforgettable views over the sea, especially on the back nine, in particular from the 11th hole. The sea breeze makes the scent of the finish line all the more enticing.

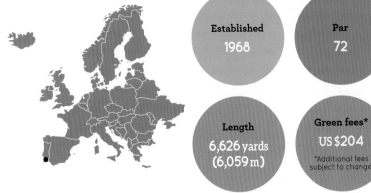

Established
1968

Par
72

Length
6,626 yards
(6,059 m)

Green fees*
US $204
*Additional fees subject to change.

Vale do Lobo Golf Club *Almansil, Portugal*

The Royal Course is considered to be Vale do Lobo's centerpiece. Designed by Rocky Roquemore based on Sir Henry Cotton's original layout, it is a very high-level (but also somewhat forgiving) course, where the European Tour has called in on two occasions for the Portugal Open, in 2002 and 2003. With perfect greens and fairways amid fig trees and stone pines, the Royal offers a balanced mix, with a variety of hole lengths, hills, water hazards and large bunkers. All this with the Atlantic Ocean in full view — and the wind that goes with it. Two holes are usually the main subject of discussion in the luxurious clubhouse. The first, with its green perched on a peninsula, is the playful 9th hole, a par 3 at 167 yards

(153 m). It goes without saying that you should aim for a soft landing or risk a watery misadventure. The other is the picturesque 235-yard (215 m) par-3 16th overlooking the ocher cliffs, which offer a stunning view. Players are almost obliged to take a short break to fully appreciate the moment. They say that this is the most photographed hole on any golf course in Portugal. That said, with the challenges in front of you, you'd better make sure you come back to your senses quickly. The range of hazards you need to avoid to keep your score from spiraling out of control include a ravine at the bottom of which lies the beach and an enormous bunker just in front of the green.

On the border of Germany and Denmark, in the north of the Wadden Sea, is an island named Sylt, which stretches out in the form of a beach 26 miles (40 km) in length. Although the location has long been prized by Germans looking to get back to nature, the southern tip, a former military base that was bombed during the Second World War, had been derelict since the 1990s. A local architect, Rolf-Stephan Hansen, had the idea of turning it into an 18-hole golf course facing the mainland. It took a year and a half to fully demolish and decontaminate the site. For

the designer, it was a case of rekindling the simple and rugged spirit of traditional links courses using everything the setting had to offer. Even though everything was manufactured from scratch, there is nothing ostentatious or ultra-modern about this course. The result is a very challenging course that is constantly striving to improve. Indeed, in 2019, half of the bunkers were turned into EcoBunkers using recycled artificial turf.

Established
2008

Par
72

Length
6,584 yards
(6,020 m)

Green fees*
US $48–108
*Additional fees
subject to change.

Budersand Sylt Golf Club   *Hörnum, Germany*

The Budersand Sylt course is perfectly in keeping with the values of a country where environmentalism has long been a central concern. This course was developed in complete harmony with nature and has found pride of place among the dunes, with its old-style, elegantly discreet charm. In golfing terms, the course quickly received very favorable reviews. The opening hole is a great example: This downhill par 4 at 418 yards (382 m) veers leftward, and there is a raised green protected by dunes on the right. Players might be hoping for a gentle start but will very quickly realize what this course has in store for them. It is a links course requiring players' full attention, especially due to the wind off the North Sea, which can be a complete game-changer around the first half of the course. Here, ending up in a good position on the fairway really is a combat sport. As many as 94 pot bunkers are mercilessly positioned around the course. The back nine is also by no means a cakewalk. The highlights of the second half are the 13th and 15th par 3s set deep in the dunes like a classic British links course. A small stream runs through the final three holes. The magnificent final sequence will almost certainly appeal to all golf lovers, as it takes inspiration from one of the most famous courses in the world: the Championship Course at Carnoustie.

Better known under the name The Hague or Royal Hague, the Koninklijke Haagsche, founded in 1893, is the oldest golf club in the Netherlands and has hosted an array of international competitions. Its current course is, however, more recent. It was designed in the 1930s by the famous architecture firm Colt, Alison & Morrison Ltd. among the dunes of Meijendel. After the Second World War, which left Europe in ruins, the club was forced to relocate, moving to Wassenaar. For golfing enthusiasts, The Hague is inextricably linked to two other neighboring courses along the Dutch coastline. The first, Noordwijkse, is set among dunes that have hosted golf for over a century, but whose current 18-hole course opened in 1970. The second, Kennemer, is an old-style links course founded in 1927 and featuring a magnificent thatched-roof clubhouse. This is where Seve Ballesteros won his first pro tournament, back in 1976.

Established
1938

Par
72

Length
6,847 yards
(6,261m)

Green fees*
US $242
*Additional fees subject to change.

Koninklijke Haagsche Golf and Country Club *Wassenaar, the Netherlands*

First things first, let's debunk some myths. Just because this course is in the Netherlands does not mean that it is not undulating or hilly. Just a few miles from the North Sea coastline, the course weaves its way through the dunes and has found a special place in Dutch golfing history. Varied, unpredictable, challenging and with new views to take in at every hole, Koninklijke Haagsche, often simply called The Hague in English, quickly became a standout course on both the national and European stages. Despite not being a coastal course, its lush setting is imbued with the spirit of a British-style links course and plays like one too. The 381-yard (348 m) par-4 hole 3 attests to this, with a rightward dogleg and a green located on the highest part of the entire course. Big hitters are advised to aim straight down the middle, while players with shorter drives should aim left to avoid the gully on the right-hand side. After that stern challenge comes the reward of hole 4, considered by many to be the most stunning and bucolic golf hole in the Netherlands. From a raised tee, players need to aim for the small green. Finally, there is no greater joy than the 18th and its narrow fairway cutting through the trees with the typical, charming clubhouse in the background. But you need to avoid the three dangerous bunkers protecting the last green before you get to sit back and enjoy a refreshing beer.

Playing ball sports at altitude is often an adventure, since you can't rely on your usual points of reference. For example, at 4,920 feet (1,500 m) above sea level, like at Crans-sur-Sierre, or at 6,560 feet (2,000 m), like at Adelboden's Golf Mountain (following spread), the lower air resistance means that the balls fly 10% further. Not only can you enjoy the breathtaking views, but you can get the satisfaction of suddenly feeling your swing get much stronger. The history of the club dates back to the very start of the 20th century. After the construction of the first nine holes, the course was extended to 18 holes by Harry Nicholson in 1928 before being more extensively remodeled in 1995 by Ballesteros. Another golfing legend, Jack Nicklaus, was called in by the directors to work on a second course, a relatively short nine-hole course requiring the utmost accuracy. The Nicklaus-Ballesteros pairing brings back plenty of great memories: In 1976, the two men tied for second place in the British Open.

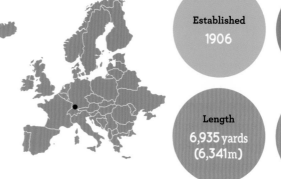

Established
1906

Par
72

Length
6,935 yards
(6,341m)

Green fees*
US $64–172
*Additional fees subject to change.

Golf Club Crans-sur-Sierre *Crans-Montana, Switzerland*

Golf isn't necessarily the first sport you would associate with Switzerland, but Crans-sur-Sierre, with its long history and almost 50-year relationship with the pro circuit, has become an unmissable stop on a golfing tour of Europe. It was on the 18th hole of this majestic course that Severiano Ballesteros hit one of the most famous shots in the history of golf, during the 1993 European Masters. Fighting for victory, the Spaniard found himself well off course, facing a wall, after a wayward shot. Despite the lack of space, Seve managed to hit a magical shot over the wall and, even though it was a completely blind shot, he almost reached the green. He then hit a wonderful chip over a bunker to get his birdie! Two years

later, the Spaniard was back, but this time as an architect, making a few modifications to the course, which has now been shortened and the greens reworked. "His" course (it was renamed in his honor) is widely considered to require great accuracy and a good all-around game. It was designed for all levels of player. The par-4 7th hole (above), at 331 yards (303 m), is an absolute must, with its unforgettable view of snowcapped mountains. And since the course is covered in snow between December and March, the winter months are the time to put away your clubs and get out your skis!

Engstligenalp Golf Mountain *Adelboden, Switzerland*

Venturing to the north of the Lofoten islands in the heart of the Arctic Circle is a feat in itself, requiring one to travel a seemingly never-ending road dotted with tunnels and bridges crossing expanses of water. Visiting in September allows you to play golf during the day and have the best chance of seeing the northern lights after dark. In July and August, you can play around the clock in the midnight sun — a unique experience in a wild and rugged setting. Located on the 68th parallel, Lofoten is the most northerly links course in the world. The greens survive by some small miracle thanks to the gulf stream. The warm current enables grass to grow after the harshest of winters, while other places along the same latitude in Alaska, Canada and Siberia are covered in permafrost, with the ground staying frozen year round. Indeed, there is something magical about Lofoten, especially since the site where the links were built houses a number of Viking graves.

Established
2005

Par
71

Length
6,662 yards
(6,092 m)

Green fees*
US $64–120
*Additional fees
subject to change.

Lofoten Links *Lofoten Islands, Norway*

"Playing golf here is like being in church. You are communing with nature." This is how the head of Lofoten Links, Frode Hov, describes this one-of-a-kind course, which gives golfers a once-in-a-lifetime opportunity. People come here not just to hit a few birdies but to play golf in a completely peerless setting. According to Jerry Mulvihill, the steward of this timeless course designed by Jeremy Turner, it offers an "extreme experience of nature." Visitors are treated to magnificent hole after magnificent hole. The highlight is the 2nd hole (above), now considered one of the most iconic in the world. It is a short par 3 with a green located on a peninsula surrounded by jagged rocks. Although players are often advised

not to get distracted by the beauty of the landscape so they can focus on their shot, that is impossible to do in Lofoten. Indeed, players should feed off it and take full advantage of the setting, which offers that much sought-after relaxation that golfers crave. The toughest hole is the 16th. It is a long par 4 with a narrow fairway stretching between the sea and a water hazard in the middle of a small peninsula. More than a few balls have been lost here along the way, but nobody ever remembers or cares. You leave Lofoten Links on such a high, your score is entirely irrelevant!

"I'd say that Thracian Cliffs is twice as good as Pebble Beach!" Gary Player certainly isn't shy when it comes to talking about his second course in Bulgaria (after BlackSeaRama). Cape Kaliakra is a truly outstanding setting, with chalk cliffs plunging down into the Black Sea. The greens around the course are nestled in the smallest nooks between sheer hillsides. South African Gary Player was the first non-American to win the Masters in 1961. He started designing golf courses in the 1980s, completing over 350 projects with his team. At Thracian Cliffs, he didn't forget to add a few of his trademark bunkers. Legend has it that he didn't stop training until he got out of the bunker and straight into the hole 100 times! Of the three courses in the area, the Lighthouse Golf Course is considered the easiest, so it can be used as a warm-up before tackling BlackSeaRama and ending with the beautiful Thracian Cliffs.

Established
2015

Par
72

Length
7,056 yards
(6,452 m)

Green fees*
US $117
*Additional fees subject to change.

Thracian Cliffs Golf and Beach Resort *Bozhurets, Bulgaria*

This is where golf and sunshine meet. At Bozhurets on the Black Sea coast, there are over 260 days of sunshine a year, so lovers of British-style links courses who like playing in drizzle might not see the appeal. Having said that, Thracian Cliffs bears more than a passing resemblance to British courses, with its occasionally rugged and wild design. This place is, however, a million miles away from those manicured, carpet-like golf courses. It stretches along towering cliffs, occasionally facing the sea, sometimes facing away, without ever really heading inland. A testament to the level of the course, it hosted the World Match Play Championship in 2013, which was the first time a European Tour event took place in

Bulgaria. Its undulating terrain provides a number of outstanding holes, which are both enjoyable and challenging, like the combination of holes 6 and 7. The 6th hole is a par 3 of 231 yards (211 m) with a raised tee on a rocky step located 130 feet (40 m) above the green on the seafront. The par-4 7th plays 378 yards (346 m), starting by the sea from a small peninsula. You need to drive at least 186 yards (170 m) over the water to reach dry land and the fairway. And to make it tougher still, the green is raised, meaning that a good second shot is a must. This hole exemplifies a course where nothing is easy.

Welcome to Acadia in the Gulf of Saint Lawrence, where the first French colonists arrived some 400 years ago to set up their cod fisheries. These dunes and cliffs on the northern coast of Cape Breton Island have been skillfully incorporated into two exceptional courses – Cabot Cliffs and Cabot Links – both highly popular in international rankings. Convinced that the outstanding setting and character of these two courses would entice golfers to the edge of Canada, the passionate golf enthusiast and visionary businessman Ben Cowan-Dewar achieved this

double success. Designed by Rod Whitman and opened in 2012, Cabot Links challenges players with constant wind gusts that sweep along the coast. Every player hopes to feel the thrill of hitting a hole in one, even though statistics show you have a 1 in 12,500 chance of making it! From the end of spring, you might even spot some whales here, since they spend the warmer months in the gulf.

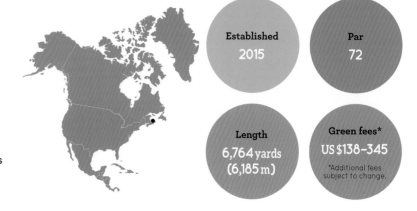

Established
2015

Par
72

Length
6,764 yards
(6,185 m)

Green fees*
US $138–345
*Additional fees subject to change.

082

Cabot Cliffs Golf Course   *Inverness, Nova Scotia, Canada*

Looking for an out-of-the-ordinary golfing destination? Look no further than Inverness in Nova Scotia. This village of around 1,000 inhabitants is close to two links courses, Cabot Cliffs and Cabot Links (following spread), which are just a few miles apart. These two courses are indisputably among the most beautiful in North America and, according to some, the world. Partly situated on an old coal mine, Cabot Links is distinctive for having a front nine that is much longer than the back nine. Among these shorter holes, the 14th is 102 yards (93 m) and heads downhill to a green perched on a cliff top, and it's absolutely stunning. It is critical to judge your power accurately and take account of the wind on this hole, which

has quickly become Cabot Links' flagship, despite stiff competition from the 16th, one of six others lining the ocean. By no means does Cabot Cliffs stand in the shadow of its older sibling. The second course was designed amid slightly more varied landscapes and terrain, with a mix of woodland, wetland and even grassland, which forced its creators to divide the front nine into an unusual combination of holes (three par 3s, three par 4s and three par 5s). The jewel in the crown of this course is the 16th hole, where you can aim over the coastline to land on the undulating green, which is magnificently raised and from which you have an incredible view of the deep blue sea.

Cabot Links Golf Course   *Inverness, Nova Scotia, Canada*

In 1954, Marilyn Monroe was here in the heart of the Rocky Mountains, shooting *River of No Return*. Her husband at the time, Joe Di Maggio, went to play golf on one of the three courses at Banff, taking full advantage of this unparalleled setting, where the vertical cliffs of Mount Rundle overlook the course and the Bow River over hundreds of yards. Perhaps the hardest thing to do here is avoid letting yourself get distracted by the scenery and, for the early birds, sharing the fairways with a passing moose, caribou or bear! The Fairmont Banff Springs hotel, inspired by a Scottish castle, adds a touch of majesty and otherworldliness to the location. Following the road northward, winding between the Rockies and passing Lake Louise, you reach another golfers' paradise: Jasper Park (following spread). Almost a century ago, it took more than 200 men and 50 teams of horses over a year to clear the site and lay the foundations for this course, which is less steep-sided than its sister course in Banff.

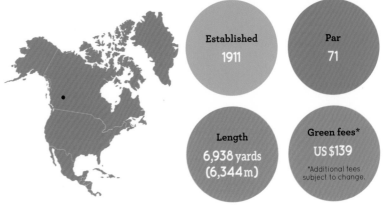

Established
1911

Par
71

Length
6,938 yards
(6,344 m)

Green fees*
US $139
*Additional fees
subject to change.

Banff Springs Golf Course *Banff, Alberta, Canada*

It is hard to imagine a more majestic theater. Playing golf with the Rocky Mountains in the background is a rare, even unique experience. Doing so at Banff Springs is extra special, given the course's worldwide renown and colorful history. The course was founded in 1911 at the impetus of Bill Thomson, a Scottish expat who learned his trade under Old Tom Morris at St. Andrews. After being extended to 18 holes in 1924, the course took on its final form thanks to Canadian master Stanley Thomson, who, with generous funding from the Canadian Pacific Railway, was able to let his dreams and imagination run wild. It is said this was the world's most expensive course at the time as well as its designer's best. Most notably, it is home to a legendary 4th hole, known as the "Devil's Cauldron." This 199-yard (182 m) par 3 starts high, and players need to cross a pond to reach a slightly raised green protected by six bunkers set against a mountainous backdrop. You really have to work to score well on this little gem. The Cauldron never opens before late May, after this part of the course has had enough sunshine to enable the grass to recover its color and strength. Some are even tempted to play one or two bad shots on purpose so they can spend a bit longer on this 200 yards of magic.

Jasper Park Golf Course *Jasper, Alberta, Canada*

Set back slightly from British Columbia's Sea to Sky Highway and offering stunning panoramas, Furry Creek boasts an exceptional view over the sea, ancient forests and snow-capped mountains. Developed 30 years ago on former mining land, Furry Creek follows the river named after a trapper-turned-prospector, crosses through the forest and finishes up on the banks of Howe Sound. Although Furry Creek closes its greens during the winter months, other nearby courses stay open all year round, including Capilano (following spread), which

was designed by Stanley Thompson and is set in the middle of a primeval forest, with the North Shore mountains in the background. In the words of one Sean Connery, who never grew tired of the stunning view over Vancouver, "there's no finer place to be on a Monday morning than the first tee at Capilano." In this wonderful city, ranked among the best places to live in the world, you can ski, sail and play golf all in the same day.

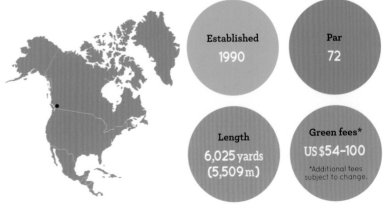

Established
1990

Par
72

Length
6,025 yards
(5,509 m)

Green fees*
US $54–100

*Additional fees
subject to change.

Furry Creek Golf and Country Club *Furry Creek, British Columbia, Canada*

As is often the case on a links course, you need to factor in the wind on this undulating course set in the middle of a centuries-old rainforest. The wind is also why players are advised to play in the morning, which tends to be a bit calmer, especially along Furry Creek's flagship par-3 14th hole. A birdie is possible at the start of the day for the most assured players. However, as the wind grows stronger in the afternoon, the 14th hole can drive players mad. A word to the wise: try to land on the right part of the green. But before you get there, you need to be on your game to avoid the bunkers at the 2nd, find the green on the 3rd, the shortest hole on the course, and take on the 4th, the course's longest hole, where you should try to

position yourself on the left side of the fairway. You'll need to accomplish all of this while not getting too distracted by the magnificent view from the 10th. There really is no time to relax at Furry Creek, as you need to be on your guard on the 12th hole too! It can be completed in one shot if you're lucky, or in many more, especially if your approach shot is not up to scratch. The other distinctive aspect of this public course is its abundant wildlife. It is not unusual to see an eagle flying overhead or to spot a deer or even a brown bear. No amount of focus can completely block out the wonder of this place.

Capilano Golf and Country Club   *Vancouver, British Columbia, Canada*   093

Over there, that's America! Because of how the border was drawn, the southern tip of Vancouver Island is a small Canadian enclave just south of the border, surrounded by the United States. It faces San Juan and Orcas Islands, on the other side of the Haro Strait, and Seattle is just a little further south. Opened in 1893, Victoria is one of the oldest golf club in Canada and still sits on its original site, where it was created by British immigrants. It expanded from 14 to 18 holes two years later and has only had three different layouts over its 130-year history, with the current one dating to the 1920s. Only the bunkers have had a more recent renovation, to make the course more competitive. The Tudor-style clubhouse lends some extra charm to the venue. The sea is visible from most of the holes, and it is not unusual to spot some seals or orcas along this sheltered coastline. Since Victoria benefits from a relatively mild microclimate, you can play here all year round, enjoying views of Vancouver's snow-capped North Shore Mountains and, further east, Mount Baker.

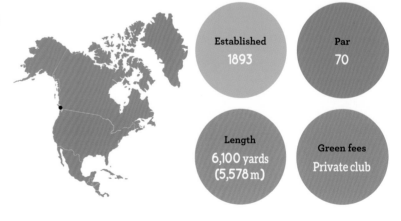

Established
1893

Par
70

Length
6,100 yards
(5,578 m)

Green fees
Private club

Victoria Golf Club   *Oak Bay, British Columbia, Canada*

The UK and Canada remain inextricably linked, and you can certainly feel it at the Victoria Golf Club. This course is not a British-style links, but it has maintained the same spirit. The Atlantic Ocean and North Sea of British links have been replaced by the Pacific Ocean, which plays a major role in making this course so enjoyable. Players have a view of the ocean from 15 of the 18 holes! Your feet are almost in the sea on seven of the holes on this course, sometimes known as "the Canadian Pebble Beach," whose greens have a reputation for being speedy. It is a relatively short course with three par 5s, five par 3s and ten par 4s, six of which are shorter than 400 yards (365 m). There are two holes in particular that catch players' attention. First, the par-4 5th hole, known as the Bay, plays

324 yards (296 m) and requires a tee shot of at least 153 yards (140 m) over the water and bank. Second, the par-4 7th (above), known as Mount Baker, plays 383 yards (350 m) and is considered to be the course's signature hole, running alongside the open ocean. This hole found fame after being the scene of miseries for Ben Hogan. The great American champion of the 1950s was a little too generous with his putting and ended up out-of-bounds. Known for the incredible quality of his stroke and nicknamed "the Wee Iceman" because of his cool head, on that day, Hogan went quietly off the rails. The magnificence and beauty of the surroundings may have been partially to blame...

Near the 14th hole at Bandon Trails is a plaque marking the exact spot where Mike Keiser decided to buy the land to turn it into a golfing paradise. His venture proved to be a roaring success. The first course, Bandon Dunes, opened in 1999. Perched on an outcrop overlooking the Pacific, its large, undulating fairways are dotted with hazards and constantly battered by wind. Three years later, Pacific Dunes opened to rave reviews with its very varied course, weaving between pines and spectacular dunes. Bandon Trails (following spread) is distinct from the other two courses: after two seafront holes, the course heads down toward a vast grassland before entering the woods, where the trees give players welcome protection from the wind. The most recent addition, Sheep Ranch, opened in 2020 and is a more rugged and stripped back course. It doesn't have any bunkers, but it does have nine cliff-top greens.

Established
2001

Par
71

Length
6,633 yards
(6,065 m)

Green fees*
US $110–450
*Additional fees subject to change.

Bandon Dunes Golf Resort (Pacific Dunes) *Bandon, Oregon, United States*

The dream of any self-respecting designer is to create a course in harmony with nature. Monumental construction works have their own charm, but this course is based on a different approach, with the holes winding around existing dunes without disturbing them and the landscape hardly touched in the creation of the fairways. This was the philosophy of Tom Doak, who found the perfect place to realize his dreams on Oregon's southern coast. Having noted that land's topography was almost identical to that of the very first golf courses in Scotland, Doak sought to create a very high-level golfing venue. According to him, "The 13th at Pacific Dunes is one of the most beautiful holes we've ever built. It was almost exactly like it is today when we found it; we just had to cap the fairway with sand so we could grow grass there." The blending of the course with the environment and surrounding elements is particularly evident on the 4th hole, a par 4 of 423 yards (387 m) — a little gem stretching along the Pacific coast that is whipped by wind and waves. Players are strongly advised to stay left, both on the fairway and on the green. Pacific Dunes immerses you in an authentic golfing experience. In a country where some courses like to dazzle and amaze at the expense of the environment, this is a real breath of fresh air!

Bandon Dunes Golf Resort (Bandon Trails) *Oregon, United States*

The Monterey peninsula was made for golf! No less than seven courses have been created here, including Cypress Point and Pebble Beach, which has become as iconic as Augusta or the Old Course at St. Andrews. Pebble Beach has only undergone minor changes since it was originally developed back in 1919 by amateur designers Jack Neville and Douglas Grant. Some improvements have been made here and there by Herbert Fowler, Alister MacKenzie, Arnold Palmer and Jack Nicklaus, who revised the 5th hole. The outstanding setting has made the course a roaring success, with its small protected greens and wonderful views of the Pacific from the 6th hole onward. The addition of a few celebrities, including Bing Crosby, who started up a tournament (later renamed the AT&T Pebble Beach Pro Am), and Clint Eastwood, who was the mayor of the neighboring city of Carmel in the 1980s, cemented the venue's legendary status, combining glamor with high-level sport. With green fees of $600 and up, mere mortals will need to raid their piggy banks to play here!

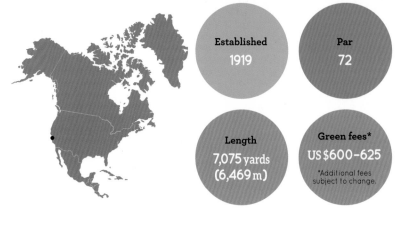

Established
1919

Par
72

Length
7,075 yards
(6,469 m)

Green fees*
US $600–625
*Additional fees subject to change.

Pebble Beach Golf Links *Pebble Beach, California, United States*

You enter Pebble Beach as if walking into a beautiful mansion with a perfectly maintained parquet floor. It takes you a few seconds to come to terms with the fact that you have set foot on some of the most hallowed ground in the world of golf. History, excellence, great views and high-level competition converge on this California peninsula. The prestige of this course also owes a lot to the fact that it has hosted the US Open on six occasions and was the venue for Tiger Woods's legendary performance in 2000. Winning the title at 12 under par, 15 shots ahead of the field, Tiger was close to perfection over the four days of the competition. Its coastal holes, from 4 to 10, are renowned for their difficulty and considered to be one of the most beautiful sequences in all of golf. This series includes the course's most iconic hole: the 7th (following spread). At just 105 yards (96 m), this par 3 with a raised tee might be the shortest on the PGA circuit, but the gusty wind makes it fiendishly difficult to find the green, with waves lapping at its edges. And since everything at Pebble Beach needs to be perfect, even the 18th hole (above), which at many courses is often simply a route back to the clubhouse, is a classic, with a narrowing fairway, beach on the left and plenty of trees to avoid, forcing you to maintain your focus right to the end.

Pebble Beach Golf Links *Pebble Beach, California, United States*

Surely every golfer dreams of playing at Cypress Point — the course described by Sandy Tatum, former president of the US Golf Association (USGA), as "The Sistine Chapel of Golf." Unlike Pebble Beach, this prestigious club on the Monterey Peninsula is one of the most exclusive in the world, with only 250 members. Legend has it that even John F. Kennedy was refused access... to the restaurant! The work of course architects Alister MacKenzie and Robert Hunter, Cypress Point was one of the first clubs to open in California prior to the golden age of golf, between

1935 and 1940. And it was Sandy Tatum once more who convinced the club to get back to basics. As a result, during its renovation in 2004, the dunes and bunkers were remodeled to reflect MacKenzie's original designs, based on old photos found in the archives. Most who have played at Cypress credit it with having the best 17 holes in the world. The 18th is only there to bring players back to the clubhouse.

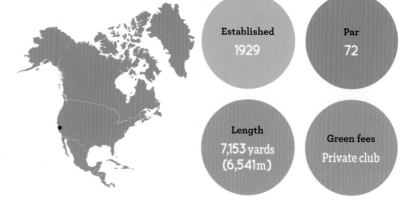

Established
1929

Par
72

Length
7,153 yards
(6,541m)

Green fees
Private club

Cypress Point Country Club   *Virginia Beach, California, United States*

To play at Cypress Point, you need to either be friends with a member or willing to spend the somewhat modest sum of $7,000 on a membership (per year, for a minimum of two years). Once that is sorted, players can enjoy a course renowned for its extraordinary bunkers. Wherever you are, the sand traps are never too far away! Strategically positioned bunkers of all shapes and sizes give Cypress a wonderful aesthetic that is in complete harmony with nature and the surrounding coastline. Players come here particularly for the magnificent series of holes 15, 16 and 17, where the noise of the waves crashing against the rocks, seals calling and birds singing immerse the lucky few who play at Cypress in a wonderfully

uproarious scene. When it comes to playing these holes, there is no time for nerves or erring over your choice of club, as you need to cross water on three separate occasions. To start, the 144-yard (132 m) par-3 15th (above) has a well-protected green, while the main dish, the par-3 16th, is 199 yards (182 m) in length. No need to look on a map to find the land route because there isn't one! Ending the series in magnificent style, both the tee and green of the 379-yard (347 m) par-4 17th are just feet away from the open ocean. Who could ask for more?

When more northernly latitudes are frozen over in midwinter, it is the perfect time to play in La Quinta. From April to November, the temperature doesn't drop below 85°F (29°C). This city in the middle of the Californian desert quickly became the refuge of Hollywood celebrities in the 1930s, which is when the first 18-hole golf course in the area opened. Today, La Quinta has a good 20 or so courses designed by top architects, including PGA West courses such as Mountain and Dunes (designed by Pete Dye), and the Quarry (designed by Tom Fazio), not to mention the many courses in Palm Springs and Palm Desert, such as the Classic Club (following spread). It's safe to say there's plenty to get through! Arnold Palmer designed a course so close to the Santa Rosa Mountains that on some holes, it feels like the mountain is rising up from the edge of the green. The clubhouse was created from a beautifully renovated hacienda dating back to the 1960s, giving the venue an extra sprinkle of charm.

Established
2005

Par
72

Length
7,552 yards
(6,906 m)

Green fees*
From US $120
*Additional fees subject to change.

SilverRock Resort *La Quinta, California, United States*

Among the plethora of courses in the Californian desert, SilverRock is one of the most popular and, at 7,552 yards (6,906 m), was one of the longest on the PGA circuit, when it was included from 2008 to 2011. This high-quality course designed by Arnold Palmer lies at the foot of the rocky Santa Rosa Mountains, whose shades of pink in the evening are unforgettably beautiful. This perfect combination of scenery and golf is extremely affordable to say the least, since this top-level course is La Quinta's municipal golf club. With six different tees available, the course is suitable for all levels and even has a short version that is only 4,542 yards (4,153 m) long. Here, the wide fairways have been planted with the famous Bermuda grass, a strong turf sometimes used in soccer stadiums. It is particularly well maintained here, making it relatively slick. Players beware: the course is peppered with more than 50 wide and deep bunkers (the most dangerous being those on holes 4 and 8) and features water hazards on no less than eight holes. This is the case for the second-to-last hole, a 236-yard (216 m) par 3, that is considered to be the course's flagship.

Classic Club *Palm Desert, California, United States*

Anyone looking to gorge themselves on golf should head to PGA West, in the Californian desert. It is the perfect complex for golf addicts, with six different courses (or four if you exclude the two reserved for members only). In any case, there's plenty of fun to be had here, especially as every course is high-end! All are the handiwork of top names: Arnold Palmer, Jack Nicklaus, Tom Weiskopf and Greg Norman. Palmer's course is famous for the last five holes at the foot of the Santa Rosa Mountains; Norman's course is considered "hard but fair"; Nicklaus designed two courses, the Private and the Tournament, featuring his signature raised tees and greens with streamlined shapes; and Tom Weiskopf's course is perhaps most appreciated by European players. Weiskopf took the principles of the Scottish links course and applied them to the middle of the desert, including the famous Swilean Bridge from St. Andrews's Old Course.

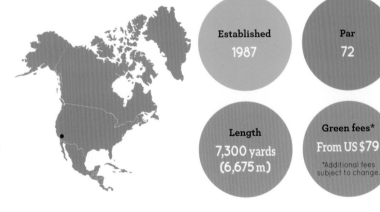

Established
1987

Par
72

Length
7,300 yards
(6,675 m)

Green fees*
From US $79

*Additional fees
subject to change.

PGA West   *La Quinta, California, United States*

"Golf is not a fair game, so why build a fair golf course?" That was the response of legendary architect Pete Dye when asked why his courses were so difficult. PGA West's Stadium Course certainly isn't an exception to the rule. It is said that even the pros complained, forcing the club's management to make some changes. Amateur players are therefore advised to keep a low profile by opting for the front tees and keep their expectations in check or risk dampening their enjoyment of this outstanding location and course that was designed for PGA competitions. PGA West is also seen as a continuation of the Stadium Course at TPC Sawgrass, also designed by Dye. The challenge is the same: Players need good distance but must stay within the course limits at all costs. It is a devilish mix of undulating fairways, huge water hazards, pot bunkers and other even more intimidating features, all surrounded by retaining walls leading to raised greens on which correct placement of the ball is key. The combination of the 17th and 18th holes before the clubhouse is wicked. The 17th (above) at PGA West, nicknamed "Alcatraz," is a copy of the peninsula green at Sawgrass, and the layout of the 18th runs the entire length of a small lake, with the green perched right on its edge.

Las Vegas may be a good 90 minutes away, but there's no shortage of excitement at Wolf Creek. It shows its true colors at the very first tee, with its downhill fairways snaking into the canyons below. The 360-degree panoramic views are fantastic. Architect Dennis Rider brilliantly succeeded in making the most of a unique natural setting in a hostile environment. He needed helicopters to move rocks and carry the many tons of earth needed to fertilize the desert and turn it green thanks to a unique irrigation system. Wolf Creek was immortalized in the 2009 video game featuring Tiger Woods. On the ground, players sometimes find themselves wishing they had superpowers to leap over the occasionally deceptive hills. Every hole offers a magnificent view. From the raised tees, the immaculate bunkers look like huge white flowers laid out on the greens. Given the overwhelming heat of the summer, the best period for playing here is either in the spring or fall.

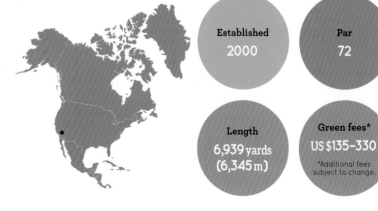

Established
2000

Par
72

Length
6,939 yards
(6,345 m)

Green fees*
US $135–330
*Additional fees
subject to change.

Wolf Creek Golf Club *Mesquite, Nevada, United States*

Welcome to Wolf Creek, where the ground is as red as the surface of Mars. Just like the scientists who hope to one day send people to the Red Planet, Wolf Creek's promoters and designers needed a hefty dose of ambition to believe that a high-level 18-hole course could ever be created here. It is an astounding course with plenty of ups and downs — a roller-coaster ride where every hole is a new adventure. Walking the course is forbidden, so a golf cart is compulsory when tackling this undulating terrain. Indeed, Wolf Creek is not just another golfing venue in an extraordinary setting, it is a high-quality course whose main asset is its diversity, with a mixture of short and long holes and some easier ones combined with tricky

doglegs. This variety is evident in the unique design of each hole and the impeccable fairways that are a real feast for the eyes. The greens are quick and challenging. When asked which hole is the signature hole, general manager Darren Stanek said that players who come here find it impossible to pick just one. In other words, all 18 holes are iconic! The simplest solution would perhaps be to go and find out for yourself...

With its many shades of blues, greens and reds, it is undoubtedly the color of earth, mountains, rocks and bunkers that dominates at Sand Hollow, Utah, surrounded by red desert and, on occasion, snow. The views from the front nine are magnificent, with the mountains of Pine Valley in the background and the Three Sisters overlooking holes 2 and 8. But that is nothing compared with the back nine and the dizzying fairways of holes 11 through 14 (hole 13 is pictured above), which flirt with the edge of a rocky plateau above a canyon carved out by the Virgin River, which flows into the Colorado. We are nestled in the heart of the most beautiful landscapes in the American West, between the Grand Canyon and the Vermilion Cliffs. If you still have some energy left, you can keep going on the club's second course, a British links-style nine-hole (which should be expanded to 18) with wide greens and fairways, fiendish bunkers and the red desert ambiance to boot!

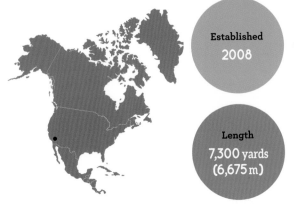

Established
2008

Par
72

Length
7,300 yards
(6,675 m)

Green fees*
From US $95
*Additional fees subject to change.

Sand Hollow Resort (Hurricane Course) *Hurricane, Utah, United States*

Visiting the Rocky Mountains and the red deserts of the American West is an experience in itself. So what about playing golf there? Designed entirely in ocher stone by former pro John Fought, Sand Hollow gives avid players the chance to try something new. This championship course is a perfect green oasis among rocks. The first half is a high-level course, while the second half is slightly less challenging but offers views straight out of the classic westerns, occasionally dizzying but always spectacular. Although holes 5 and 18 are deemed the most difficult, the par-3 15th was quickly recognized as the course's signature hole. Its nicknamed the "Devil's Throat," which makes it clear what lies ahead: From the tee surrounded by rocks, players aim to reach the two-tiered green by flying over a long creek ready to swallow errant golf balls, never to be seen again. Hitting a good shot here is an unforgettable thrill, especially as the wind likes to get involved too. Players who have succeeded attest that landing near the flag on the 15th at Sand Hollow is a little taste of heaven. In any case, it is certainly better than going down to the devil!

If the ghosts of the Fownes, a father and son team, returned to haunt Oakmont, they probably wouldn't recognize the course they designed back in 1903. Since then, no less than seven architects have worked on modifying this legendary course. This involved tens of thousands of trees being uprooted and the number of bunkers being reduced from 350 to just over 200, which is still a significant amount. The club remains firmly wedded to its centuries-old traditions and greets the digitization of our modern world with the utmost reticence. At Oakmont, you can only use your phone in the changing rooms or in your car in the parking lot. Computers are not allowed in the clubhouse. Wearing the proper attire is taken very seriously too. The dress code requires collared shirts or mock turtlenecks and trousers, and jeans are not allowed. Although shorts are tolerated, make sure you check their length! A gap greater than an inch between the knee and the bottom of the shorts is a sacrilege.

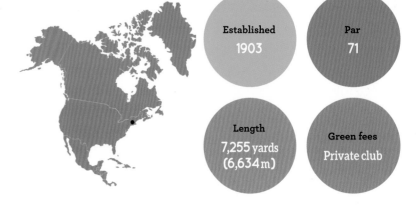

Established
1903

Par
71

Length
7,255 yards
(6,634 m)

Green fees
Private club

Oakmont Country Club *Pittsburgh, Pennsylvania, United States*

In 2025, Oakmont will host its 10th US Open – a record that says a lot about the quality of this course, as does the list of players who have triumphed here. Aside from Sam Parks Jr., every other winner has been inducted into the Hall of Fame. You can't luck your way into winning here, since this course, created over a century ago by the Fownes family, forces players to play their very best and shines a light on their strengths (and weaknesses). Indeed, the expressions used by players and the media to describe this course, strangely cut in two by Route 76, are enough to make you want to stay huddled inside the hushed surroundings of the chic clubhouse with a nice whisky: "the Torture Chamber," "penal-style course design,"

"brutal" and "evil genius." The course is known for (among other things) its narrow fairways, aggressive roughs and quick greens, which are enough to give any player a headache as they approach the flag. It is also impossible to talk about Oakmont without mentioning the two uniquely shaped bunkers: the first is Church Pews, located between holes 3 and 4, where thin strips of sand separated by small rounded mounds of turf resemble the eponymous church seating, and the second is Big Mouth, protecting the 17th hole, designed using the same principle. It goes without saying that avoiding these is strongly advised, or you may never get out again!

Merion may not have the majesty of Augusta or the coastal beauty of Pebble Beach, but in the opulent suburbs of Philadelphia, Hugh Wilson created a unique golf course on land previously reserved for cricket. A complete novice in course design, Wilson spent seven months visiting the most beautiful clubs in the British Isles to understand what makes them so special. This is what helps to give every hole on this compact course its specific personality and distinctiveness. Despite being inland, it bears more than a passing resemblance to a links course. It

was renovated in 2014 to better suit the modern game and its big hitters. The second course, the West, is the perfect warm-up for tackling the East. Merion is famous for using red wicker baskets (orange on the back nine) instead of flags. The idea may have been taken from English shepherds, who used to keep their lunches wrapped in wicker bundles. Replacing flags can, nonetheless, have some disadvantages when the wind starts to pick up.

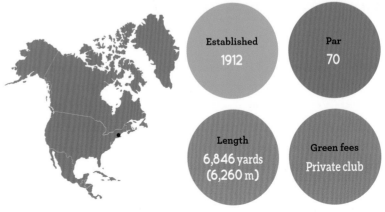

Established
1912

Par
70

Length
6,846 yards
(6,260 m)

Green fees
Private club

Merion Golf Club (East Course)

Ardmore, Pennsylvania, United States

It is often said that the East Course at Merion is a play in three acts. Act 1: six long, relatively intimidating holes. Act 2: six more entertaining holes, which nonetheless keep players on their toes. Act 3: to finish, six holes considered to be about as tough as golf gets. This is the relentless challenge set by the course, which has hosted a great many international competitions since the start of the last century, including the US Open on five occasions. Some players, especially amateurs, think that it is more difficult than Augusta. To survive, you need plenty of tactical good sense in the face of hugely varied holes, denser vegetation than on California courses and bunkers with very specific designs known here as "white faces."

When it comes to history and traditions, Merion really means business. It has been the stage of some unforgettable battles, including the one between Lee Trevino and Jack Nicklaus in a playoff at the 1971 US Open. The duel began with a touch of tomfoolery: In an attempt to relax (or jokingly put off his rival), Trevino produced a rubber snake, one of his daughter's toys that he had found in his bag. And since Trevino ended up winning, that plastic snake, which played no role in the outcome, went down in the history books.

Governed by deep-rooted traditions and some bizarre rules, including a ban on photos and cell phones, the legend of Augusta lies, above all, in its course of ultra-fast greens and narrow fairways, where every hole is named after a tree or flower (juniper, magnolia, olive and so on). It owes its reputation especially to the famous elbow-shaped combination of three holes, 11, 12 and 13, nicknamed "Amen Corner" in 1958 by renowned golfing journalist Herbert Warren Wind, since you need a miracle to bring you through it unscathed. Hole 12 (above) is a nightmare in itself,

as six-time Augusta-winner Jack Nicklaus attested: "It is an almost gentle par 3 if there is no wind. But with the wind, it is one of the hardest holes you can get." For the champions, getting the better of Amen Corner gives you a shot at wearing that famous green blazer awarded to the winner of the Masters, and it also means you'll be welcome to play here for the rest of your life.

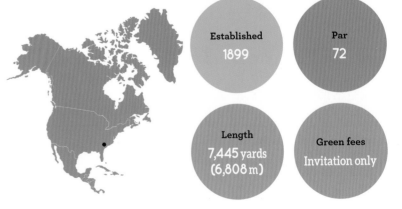

Established
1899

Par
72

Length
7,445 yards
(6,808 m)

Green fees
Invitation only

Augusta National Golf Club   *Augusta, Georgia, United States*

Augusta is all about luxury, tranquility and exquisite touches. And it is ultra-private too! Rather than a simple club, this is a class apart governed by centuries-old traditions. It only has some 300 members, who have all proven themselves worthy of the honor and who enjoy the privilege of playing here in exchange for a membership fee of around $50,000. If you really want to feel at home, you'd better have been a hit on Wall Street, like Warren Buffet, or managed a company of the caliber of Microsoft, like Bill Gates. President Dwight Eisenhower was a loyal Augusta member until his death in 1969. He even spent time in a cabin located on the course itself, just in front of the 10th tee. In exceptional circumstances, members,

who must wear a green jacket whenever they are on the premises and not playing, are allowed to invite a friend to play on the most famous and prestigious greens in North American golf. The course is renowned both for its traps and its beauty, especially in springtime, when the trees, flowers and bushes lining the course are in full bloom. Spring is also when the Masters takes place. It is the only Major tournament always held at the same venue, which is yet another reason why Augusta is so special.

Unlike the Teeth of the Dog, where Pete Dye simply harnessed what nature had to offer, he started with a clean slate at Sawgrass: an unappealing area of marshland bought symbolically for just one dollar. Once drained and developed, this course, built to be the permanent host of the Players Championship, has become a favorite training venue among top players. Pete and Alice Dye were given two main instructions: make the course accessible to a large number of players, and design "the world's most democratic" course in terms of playing level. Dye may have mixed up "democratic" with "demonic," as in its first year, even greats like Nicklaus failed to make the cut. Dye had to revise his plans and iron out some of the tougher sections. Any golfer is welcome to play at Sawgrass as long as they pay the $600 green fee. If they have a bad day, they can always find solace in the famous barber's chair, where those who fall victim to the course can air their grievances.

Established
1982

Par
72

Length
6,671 yards
(6,100 m)

Green fees*
From US $450
*Additional fees
subject to change.

TPC Sawgrass (Stadium Course) *Ponte Vedra Beach, Florida, United States*

Playing tennis at the USTA National Tennis Center is a very similar experience to playing golf at TPC Sawgrass, allowing amateurs to walk in the footsteps of the pros. Anyone who manages to finish their round at TPC without breaking a sweat, losing any balls or being driven a little mad must be a fantastic golfer! Here, everything has been done to confound visitors and champions alike on a course based on a simple and cruel philosophy: consistently play the right shot or suffer the consequences. This philosophy is embodied by the 17th hole. This 137-yard (125 m) par 3 quickly became one of the most famous and challenging holes in the world of golf, with its racket-shaped green perched on a tiny peninsula.

Every year, 100,000 balls end up in the water. This hole also gained legendary status after being the scene of some unforgettable shots, including the hole in one by Fred Couples in 1999, with the ball going straight into the hole from the tee shot, like a slam dunk in basketball. And above all, it was the site of Tiger Woods's 60-foot (18 m) putt in 2001, described by one TV commentator as "better than most" as the ball gently meandered in an S-shaped route across the green before finding the hole. In 1998, Steve Lowery didn't have the same luck when a seagull flew in and grabbed his ball straight off the green.

Ranked among the top 20 courses for over half a century, Seminole is the crowning glory of Donald Ross, who started out as an apprentice under the brilliant Old Tom Morris at St. Andrews. The show begins at this club before you even set foot on the course, with its penchant for secrecy and its strong attachment to its old traditions, including its members' very British-style welcome, the magnificent cathedral-like changing rooms and the varnished wooden lockers. The caddies at Seminole have assisted the finest players and the world's political and economic elite. When someone pointed out to Donald Ross that the stunning pink stucco clubhouse didn't have a view of the sea, he responded with exasperation: "This is a golf club, not a beach club." However well-renowned it may be, Seminole has always shunned publicity and the limelight. The first time cameramen were allowed to tread the pink gravel pathways was in May 2020, during an exhibition match to help fund research to combat COVID-19.

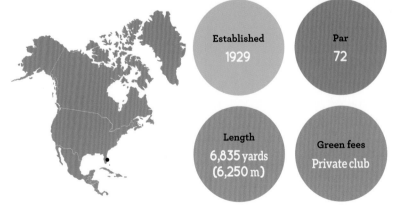

Established
1929

Par
72

Length
6,835 yards
(6,250 m)

Green fees
Private club

Seminole Golf Club *Juno Beach, Florida, United States*

Renowned for being one of America's most selective clubs, the course at Seminole Golf Club remains nonetheless an inexhaustible subject of discussion between experts and enthusiasts alike. While this windy and unexpectedly undulating course is underestimated by some and overestimated by others, it presents an undoubtedly very high-level challenge. Seminole is a crafty course that weaves among the palm trees, with holes positioned in every direction, huge stretches of sand along the fairways and plenty of elegantly shaped bunkers. Granted, they are not that deep, but since there are so many, you have to be the embodiment of Jack Nicklaus or Tiger Woods to get around the course without ending up in one of

them. Broad stretches of water (especially on the 10th, 11th and 15th holes), whose design nicely reflects that of the bunkers, spice things up on this coastal course, which gets really close to the shoreline in the final section. Undulating and varied in their design, Seminole's greens are renowned for their difficulty. It is impossible to pinpoint a single iconic hole since opinions differ so much — a sign of the all-around quality of the course and another inexhaustible subject of debate among the lucky few to have played at Seminole.

With over 70 courses across the archipelago, Hawaii has become a genuine golfing destination with varied options depending on the island, with some along the coast and others, like this one, deep in the rainforest. It so resembles a set for *Jurassic Park*, you could be forgiven for expecting a dinosaur to jump out at any moment. The magnificent amphitheater created by the Ko'olau mountains and the imposing Mount Olomona add to the ambiance. The oldest club on Oahu is the Moanalua Golf Club, a nine-hole course located close to Pearl Harbor and dating back to 1898, the year the archipelago was annexed by the United States. One of the most popular clubs along the coast is Kapalua Resort on Maui, which has hosted various international tournaments across its two courses: the Bay, famous for its 17th hole overlooking the ocean, and the Plantation, infinitely undulating and with most of the tees downhill, allowing you to unleash every last bit of power when driving the ball.

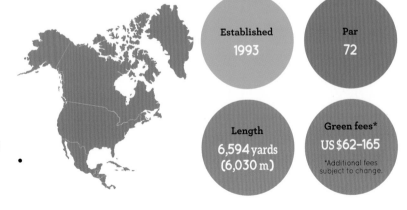

Established
1993

Par
72

Length
6,594 yards
(6,030 m)

Green fees*
US $62–165
*Additional fees
subject to change.

Royal Hawaiian Golf Club *Oahu, Hawaii, United States*

This spectacular, undulating course exudes a jungle atmosphere. It is located in the heart of the Maunawili Valley on the island of Oahu amid a meandering rainforest full of royal palms, banana trees and acacias. Much loved by former US President Bill Clinton, the course is lined by crystal-clear waters, including the course's most emblematic hole, the par-3 2nd, which plays 187 yards (171 m). Designed by father-and-son team Pete and Perry Dye in 1994, the course was later updated by former world number one Greg Norman, aka The Shark. Players are advised to take the very high humidity into account. Indeed, the greens are so slow that some say they seem like Velcro! The fairways, narrower on the front nine and wider on the back nine, are often dense and unforgiving. The variety of situations players find themselves in is so vast, it is often said that you need to use every club in your bag to complete a round. Be careful not to slip! With an average of almost 200 days of rainfall every year, some parts of the course can be muddy. It is well worth checking the weather forecast before deciding when to play. Having said that, playing amid a sudden downpour, if just for a few holes, is all part of the challenge and ambiance.

For 10 years or so, Mexico has been a first-choice golfing destination thanks to the construction of huge resorts in collaboration with well-known course designers. The outstanding locations along the coastline of Baja California include El Cardinal in Diamante, designed by Tiger Woods (another project is also in the pipeline). He took inspiration from the Californian courses so dear to his heart and created a layout among the dunes that offers a maximum of strategic choices. Another legend, Jack Nicklaus, designed Puerto Cabos, the Cove Club (Ocean) and Quivira along with other Mexican courses. It took nearly eight years to complete the monumental works among the dunes and rocky outcrops occasionally rising more than 300 feet (100 m) above the waves, making this Baja California's most coastal course. Quivira's signature 5th hole (following spread) is considered to be one of Jack Nicklaus's very best designs.

Established
2009

Par
72

Length
7,100 yards
(6,492 m)

Green fees*
US $160
*Additional fees subject to change.

Diamante Dunes Golf Course *Cabo San Lucas, Baja California, Mexico*

At the heart of Baja California's incredibly luxurious and aptly named Dunes Resort is a top course, possibly Mexico's best if the rankings are to be believed. Overlooking the Pacific Ocean, the course was designed by US champion Davis Love III (20 PGA titles and a USPGA title) and has been greeted with unanimous praise. Its success lies in how well it fits in with its natural environment and, of course, in how challenging it is to play, mainly due to the great variety of holes. It could be compared to legendary courses like Pebble Beach (a little further north on the Californian coast) or even St. Andrews (Scotland), only without the rain. With its wide fairways and very fast greens, the second half of the Dunes is

undoubtedly a little more spectacular and challenging. Some even confidently say that this back nine is one of the best in the world! This includes the combination of holes 12 and 13. The first is a wonderful, long, uphill par 3 with a green surrounded by bunkers. It is followed by a par 5 nestled between dunes to the right and stretches of sand to the left. Making it to the green is just part of the enjoyment. Once you look up and take in your surroundings, everything else pales into insignificance!

Quivira Golf Club *Cabo San Lucas, Baja California, Mexico*

Corales can pride itself on being the first club in the Dominican Republic to be featured on the US PGA Tour, in 2018. Golf is distinct in being governed by geographical area rather than by a single international body like, for instance, the ATP in men's tennis. As a result, there is also a European PGA circuit (known as the European Tour, with 40 or so tournaments), which has expanded its borders to the Middle East, as well as the PGA's Asian Tour. There is a similar division between the American and European tours on the women's side (with the LPGA and Ladies European Tour). Nevertheless, these independent circuits do share some common ground in the world rankings, which can be used to determine an overall classification and a list of tournament entries. At the sport's pinnacle are the Majors, an unofficial, historic label, which in the men's game includes the British Open, the USPGA, the US Open and the Masters, while the women's game has five Major tournaments.

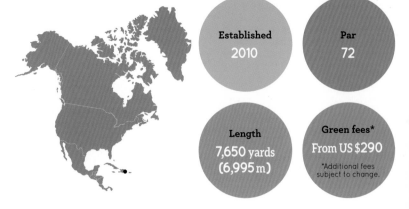

Established
2010

Par
72

Length
7,650 yards
(6,995 m)

Green fees*
From US $290

*Additional fees
subject to change.

Corales Golf Course *Punta Cana, Dominican Republic*

Apart from the blazing sun that beats down on the course for much of the day, Corales exudes the atmosphere of a Scottish links course, designed along similar jagged coasts with equally gale-force winds. Opened in 2010, the course was designed by Tom Fazio, who always strives to find the balance between risk and reward! He took full advantage of the cliffs, coves, coral rocks and inland lakes to test skilled players to their fullest, without forgetting that golf is ultimately about enjoyment. The fairways are wide, with five different tees available. The first coastal holes (six in total) begin at the end of the front nine, with greens perched on the cliff top, offering unobstructed views of the coastline and the Caribbean. The wind starts to become a factor from hole 7, a par 5 with a raised, exposed green. But the real highlight of the course is unquestionably the Devil's Elbow at the end of the back nine, named in reference to the curve of the coastline around the last three holes. The 17th plays 213 yards (195 m) as it skirts along the cliff, while the final hole, a par 4 at 501 yards (458 m), has a rightward dogleg that tempts players to hit over the water on calm days, but a hefty swing is needed if you are to make it across intact — a monumental challenge. You can't escape the devil, even in paradise!

Pete Dye designed three courses at Casa de Campo, but Teeth of the Dog is undoubtedly his masterpiece and one of his best works after TPC Sawgrass. During the works, Dye and Alice, his wife and collaborator, lived in a bungalow near the 7th hole. Teeth of the Dog is emblematic of Dye's style, which the excellent amateur player and former insurance broker has developed since becoming a course architect in the 1970s. He took inspiration from his father, who created a nine-hole course on the family's farmland, and above all from the Scottish links courses he studied during a trip in 1963. This is how he forged his own style during the 1970s and 1980s, when courses were becoming increasingly standardized. At the time of his death in early 2020, he had designed more than 120 courses around the world, combining the links aesthetic with the principles of target golf. Pete Dye influenced a whole generation of designers, including Tom Doak, Bill Coore and Robert Von Hagge.

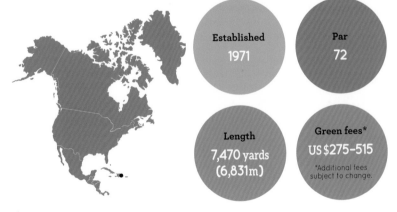

Established
1971

Par
72

Length
7,470 yards
(6,831m)

Green fees*
US $275–515
*Additional fees subject to change.

Casa de Campo (Teeth of the Dog) *La Romana, Dominican Republic*

The famous words of the legendary Pete Dye tell you everything you need to know about how highly the US architect thought of this course, opened in 1971 and updated in 2005: "For Teeth of the Dog, I created 11 holes and God took care of the other seven." The course, which owes its name to the jagged coral rocks on which it was built, is the result of two years of tireless effort on the part of more than 300 workers, who dug, scraped and shaped the coastline to create what would become one of its creator's finest works. The seven holes facing the Caribbean are a real feast for the senses. They also require maximum accuracy and focus. The famous "sink or swim" nature of Dye's courses sees alternating doglegs, small greens and vicious bunkers. The distinctiveness of Teeth of the Dog comes from its coastal holes, where the sea is a prominent feature. On four of the holes, players are almost wading into the water, unlike most links courses, which are usually positioned among dunes or on cliff tops. The award for best hole goes to the par-3 5th (above), which always proves popular with players. Players should bear in mind that the temperature and humidity rise a little in the less windy inland section, making the greens slightly spongier and, as a result, not as quick.

Mike Keiser and Ben Cowan-Dewar share a passion for golf and enticing enthusiasts from the world over to some of the planet's most remote and beautiful locations. Fresh from their success at Bandon Dunes and Cabot Links, respectively, the American billionaire and Canadian businessman teamed up on a number of other projects before setting themselves to the task of finding the ideal, untouched location for year-round golf. Leaving the coasts of Oregon and Nova Scotia behind, and after four years of searching, they set their sights on the volcanic island of Saint Lucia, where they stumbled across huge areas of land perfectly suited to the minimalism so dear to designers Bill Coore and Ben Crenshaw. There was also enough room to build a luxury resort. As Keiser often likes to point out, "One course is a curiosity. Two courses is a destination." Cabot Point seems unlikely to remain unaccompanied for long.

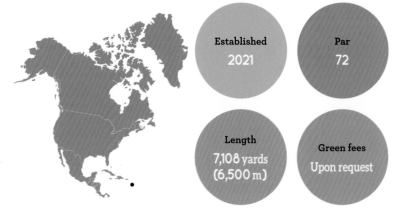

Established
2021

Par
72

Length
7,108 yards
(6,500 m)

Green fees
Upon request

Cabot Saint Lucia Golf Resort (Cabot Point) *Point Hardy, Saint Lucia*

Before it even opened, Cabot Point had all the signs of being a must visit. The résumés of its two promoters, Mike Keiser and Ben Cowan-Dewar, left people in little doubt about what to expect. Outside of magazines that specialize in golf, there has rarely been so much talk in the press about a new golf course, with stories running in the *New York Times*, *Forbes* and the *Globe and Mail*. Such was the level of interest in Cabot Point, even before anyone had even hit a ball there. Far away from the hustle and bustle of the tourist areas, Cabot Point is situated on a coastline ravaged by the waves and with undulating terrain and dense vegetation. Strong believers in a philosophy of planning layouts in harmony with their surroundings, designers Bill Coore and Ben Crenshaw had everything they needed to design this wild course. Players never lose sight of the Caribbean's turquoise waters, and seven of the holes run along the shoreline. The topography of Saint Lucia reminded the designers of Kapalua, Hawaii, where they had designed their first course together, reveling in creating holes that force players to hit over water. At Cabot Point, the 16th and 17th, both par 3s, do exactly that. According to Coore, the 16th hole in particular is likely to give players some thrills. In the words of the specialist himself: "You'll stand on a tee and the waves are going to be crashing... It's off-the-charts spectacular."

King Hassan II took a keen interest in golf in the late 1960s, when his doctor told him to stop playing tennis. The king wanted a course close to his palace in Rabat and went looking for the best architect around. He was given the name of Robert Trent Jones, who had already designed more than 100 courses and, supposedly, a putting green at the White House and a hole at Camp David for US President Dwight Eisenhower. Jones created a royal complex amid the lush vegetation lining the fairways. In total, he designed 45 holes for Dar Es Salam (meaning "the house of peace" in Arabic), which is made up of the Bleu course, with quick greens and rolling fairways, and the more challenging Rouge course, among others. Based on designs dug out from Jones's archive, a major renovation of the flagship course was completed in 2018 to significantly expand its greens and reestablish its original spirit.

Established
1971

Par
73

Length
7,329 yards
(6,702 m)

Green fees*
US $88–119
*Additional fees subject to change.

Royal Golf Dar Es Salam (Rouge) *Rabat, Morocco*

The world-class Rouge course at the Royal Golf Dar Es Salam lies in the heart of a cork oak forest peppered with cypresses and palm trees. One of the heads of the European Tour, Keith Pelley, waxes lyrical about this wondrous botanical garden of a venue, which in his view is the most beautiful on the circuit. The Hassan II Trophy, founded the same year as the club itself, has been won by top players in the past, including Payne Stewart, Colin Montgomerie, Vijay Singh, Sam Torrance and Ernie Els. The Ladies European Tour also stops off here during the same week, making it one of the very few mixed tournaments on the professional circuit. All these champions have tackled this course designed by Robert Trent Jones Sr., which is based on the ability of a player to take risks. At each hole, a player must decide whether to go for "a tricky par or an easy bogey." The course at Rabat bears all the hallmarks of this design genius: fairways with doglegs, huge bunkers and raised and complex greens. The Roman columns (above), transported here from the archeological site at Volubilis and positioned between holes 11 and 12, add either a historic or tacky touch, depending on your taste. In any case, the course's most famous hole is undoubtedly the 9th — a par 3 with a green located on a small island surrounded by flamingos. Absolutely magical!

The strong desire to create a golf club in Durban became apparent after the First World War, when the city grew into a popular seaside resort. Built on former swampland, it experienced some teething problems due to repeated flooding. It is now a reflection of the city: a perfect blend of the old and the modern, with its Dutch-style clubhouse and, in the background, the superb Moses Mabhida stadium built for the 2010 FIFA World Cup. Its architecture takes inspiration from the South African flag, with its imposing arch symbolizing unity and holding up a funicular railway. From the top, 345 feet (105 m) above the ground, you can look down on the neighboring districts and the country club's greens. On a clear day, you can almost make out its twin club, Beachwood, on the other side of the Blue Lagoon. With its long and narrow fairways, this is a challenging links course that is aligned with the runway of the nearby Virginia airport.

Established
1922

Par
72

Length
6,733 yards
(6,157 m)

Green fees*
US $28–56

*Additional fees subject to change.

Durban Country Club   *Durban, South Africa*

Having hosted the South African Open on 17 occasions and now being included on the European Tour, the Durban Country Club has earned itself the reputation of a high-level golf course. It is worth remembering that this is a pro course in a country that has bestowed a wealth of champions on the world of golf. Designed by George Waterman and L.B. Walters and revamped by local legend Gary Player, this course is known for unpredictable bounces on its fairways, reflecting the features of some of the great Scottish courses. The first half of the course is gently undulating and is set amid a sea of tropical plants, each one more fragrant than the next. For some, the first five holes at Durban represent quite simply one of the toughest opening series in the world of golf. The par-4 1st hole is 427 yards (390 m) and haunts the dreams of even some of the most experienced players. Many also come to Durban to test their mettle on the curved 3rd hole, a par 5 of 505 yards (462 m). The fairway is lined on both sides by very dense bushes and has a bunker halfway along the left side. And if things weren't already tough enough, the green is very closely protected by two more bunkers lying in wait for wayward balls, swallowing up many hopes along the way.

The icing on the cake of this highlight reel is the extreme 19th hole (following spread)! It is a point of pride that it is the longest and highest par 3 in the world. Players drive from a tee a full 1,300 feet (400 m) above the green, which is shaped like the African continent. The tee, at the summit of Hanglip Peak, is only accessible by helicopter. The 5,905-foot (1,800 m) altitude gives you a considerable helping hand. The 20 or so seconds it takes the ball to fall down to Earth seem to last an eternity. You have to keep your eye on the person on lookout waving their arms to signal that it has landed safely! Fortunately mulligans are permitted, but goodness knows how many balls have been lost in the surrounding bush among the zebras and gazelles. Nestled in the heart of the private Entabeni Reserve, the golf course's neighbors are another very select club: lions, buffaloes, elephants, leopards and rhinos, otherwise known as the "Big Five." Limpopo, much loved by Rudyard Kipling, is one of South Africa's poorest regions, but it it home to an impressive wealth of wildlife.

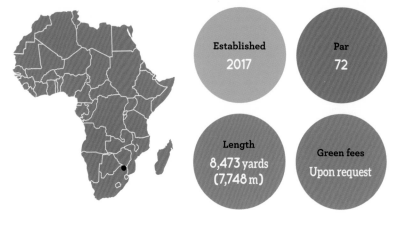

Established
2017

Par
72

Length
8,473 yards
(7,748 m)

Green fees
Upon request

Legend Golf and Safari Resort *Limpopo, South Africa*

Is it possible for cold, hard marketing to coexist alongside history and tradition? This debate could go on long into the night at countless clubhouse bars around the world. Investors in the Legend Golf and Safari answered this question with a resounding and unambiguous "yes." The result is this multifaceted club, whose principal course, the Signature, was designed by 18 different champions, some retired and some still playing, including Bernhard Langer, Justin Rose, Sergio Garcia, Raphaël Jacquelin, Vijay Singh and Ian Woosnam to name but a few. With wide fairways and manicured greens, this course also stands out for its length: 8,473 yards (7,748 m) in total from the back tees. There is also a second course

with ten holes that are exact replicas of classic par 3s from some of the greatest golf courses around the world. Amid the lush setting of Limpopo, you can drive from the 10th tee at Pine Valley, try to reach the green at the 12th and 16th holes at Augusta and shoot for a par on the 11th at St. Andrews. More conservative players may consider this as more of a theme park than a genuine course, but there can be no arguing about how much fun it is, especially when you consider the fabulous scenery.

Legend Golf and Safari Resort   *Limpopo, South Africa*

Many moons ago, the Fancourt family settled at the foot of the Outeniqua Mountains, building an elegant home that soon came to be known as Blanco House. A century and plenty of twists and turns later, the manor was turned into a luxury hotel, but it remains unchanged, nestled in a little corner of paradise, alongside a popular links course that hosts pro circuit tournaments as well as two other courses. Montagu and Outeniqua also score very highly in the rankings. Indeed, both of these courses have plenty to appreciate. Montagu, a par 72 at 7,343 yards (6,714 m), also designed by Gary Player, is noted for being a particularly fast course. Outeniqua, a par 72 at 6,903 yards (6,312 m), was designed for more relaxed play. That said, there are still plenty of challenges. No fewer than 11 holes are surrounded by water hazards. So what do the three courses at Fancourt have in common? They are all maintained to an exceptionally high quality.

Established
2000

Par
72

Length
7,579 yards
(6,930 m)

Green fees
Invitation only

Fancourt (The Links) *George, South Africa*

Gary Player himself sees this course as his biggest success as an architect. The South African golfing legend, one of just five players to have won all four Majors at least once, knows what he's talking about. Having become a designer, the great champion and his team have worked together since 1980 to build more than 300 courses around the world. Fancourt's the Links course, created entirely from scratch, was inspired by Scottish courses. According to Player, "It has been designed to make golfers feel as though they were at Ballybunion, Dornoch, or St. Andrews with rolling fairways, pot bunkers, big greens, high rough, and a seascape appearance." The outcome certainly lived up to his expectations: a high-level course intended above all for very good golfers. As a testament, it was swiftly added to the professional circuit, hosting the prestigious President's Cup in 2003, just three years after it opened. Here, players with a double-figure handicap might find it tough going. Bunkers and water hazards abound, from the undulating par-3 2nd hole to the deceptively tricky par-5 18th, on an often very compact course. Despite its beautiful setting, at the Links there is not a moment to relax.

In 2000, the construction of this golf course led to the discovery and excavation of caves that were inhabited by our ancestors some 200,000 years ago. The Big Cave and the Point of Human Origins, located just below the greens, likely helped save humanity from extinction. *Homo sapiens* took refuge there during the long ice age that gripped the Earth, and they were able to survive on the abundant edible plants and shellfish. This also explains why the location was named Mossel Bay ("mossel" means mussel in Afrikaans) by explorers in the 17th century. Following the path that runs along the coast brings you to the Cape St. Blaize lighthouse, which overlooks the natural pools at Die Poort. Peaceful at low tide, they can be dangerous when the sea comes in. Mossel Bay is the gateway to the world-famous Garden Route, which runs along the superb beaches, lakes and lagoons hidden amid the dense forest.

Established
2006

Par
72

Length
6,350 yards
(5,806 m)

Green fees*
From US $54
*Additional fees subject to change.

Pinnacle Point Golf and Beach Resort *Mossel Bay, South Africa*

This is a golf course that absolutely lives up to its name. Opened not too long ago, in 2006, Pinnacle Point Golf and Beach Resort soon reached the upper echelons of the world's most beautiful courses. Halfway between Cape Town and Port Elizabeth, this par 72 is lined with very dense and fragrant scrub known as fynbos. It has no fewer than seven holes facing the Indian Ocean, four of which are perched on a cliff top. The high point of this links course designed by architect Peter Matkovich and Darren Clarke, winner of the 2011 British Open, is hole 13. A par 3 of just 137 yards (125 m), players need to drive over a gorge to reach the green, the back of which falls steeply into the ocean below. The view from here is

outstanding, and people have even spotted dolphins and whales passing by in the distance. However, before reaching these coastal holes, players need to tackle three uphill holes, which give them the chance to find their feet before taking on the most spectacular and interesting part of the course. Replete with 80 bunkers in all, they say that this course is an excellent arbiter of one's skills. As is often the case by the sea, you can't let the unpredictability of the wind get the better of you. At Pinnacle, if you get close to your handicap (or better it), you have undoubtedly mastered a very fine course.

Perhaps the Choo Tjoe, an old 1930s steam train that ran along South Africa's famed Garden Route, might one day be put back into service so that the region's three exceptional golf courses, Pinnacle, Fancourt and Pezula can be connected once more. Until that time, a rather unusual type of visitor is often seen on the course: a troop of baboons visibly enjoying their surroundings on the greens alongside the environmentally friendly irrigation system protecting the fynbos — emblematic of South Africa's shrubland — lining the course. The course sweeps down toward the Knysna Lagoon, renowned for being the entrance to the world's most dangerous port. Into this vast estuary flow no less than five rivers, descending from the Outeniqua Mountains into the sea. The views over the ocean from the outcrops known as the Knysna Heads are spectacular. The Feather Bed Nature Reserve, devastated by fire in 2017, has since regained all of its splendor, its colors contrasting beautifully with the turquoise waters of the lagoon.

Established
2001

Par
72

Length
6,521 yards
(5,963 m)

Green fees*
US $54–80
*Additional fees subject to change.

Pezula Golf House   *Knysna, South Africa*

The small town of Knysna has a special place in the hearts of golfers. A few miles from the center, the Pezula Championship Golf Course has earned itself an excellent reputation in the two short decades since its founding. You could almost say that it is a multi-story course. Designers Ronald Fream and David Dale perfectly harnessed the rolling topography of this area of headland overlooking the sea, so much so that you need to take long wooden stairs between some holes, giving the course a certain charm. Players should ensure their seat belts are securely fastened on this rollercoaster course with a breathtaking variety of holes, especially in the first half. On the back nine, the par-5 13th hole provides immense enjoyment as it rolls downhill to the 14th (above), Pezula's magnificent signature hole. This cliff-top par 4, which takes an abrupt turn in the final quarter, becomes particularly engrossing near the green. Indeed, it isn't surrounded by a few bunkers as much as it is engulfed in a desert! Planning a careful approach is essential if you don't want to spend more time than you bargained for on this hole. That said, getting stuck in the sand is a great excuse to take in the view a little bit longer.

Until a few years ago, the only way to get to the Île aux Cerfs was in a traditional dugout canoe. Motorboats now ferry visitors and golfers from Trou d'Eau Douce to this iconic islet just off the coast of Mauritius, but that is just the start of the adventure. Opened in 2003, the course's 94 acres (38 ha) cover almost the entire island, also making it the second biggest course in Mauritius. On the other side of the lagoon, in a less wild setting, the Anahita Golf Club (following spread) is another of Mauritius's well-renowned idyllic courses. Île aux Cerfs' 18 holes and wide fairways are built on the site of an old sugar cane plantation. It was designed by the champion golfer Ernie Els, who has proved just as successful as an architect as he was on the greens. Among the six holes looking out onto the lagoon, the par-5 4th, where the wind always seems to blow into your face, is the standout. You definitely need to get your driver out here, and to get a birdie, you should attack the green from left to right.

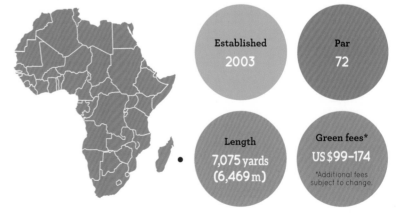

Established
2003

Par
72

Length
7,075 yards
(6,469 m)

Green fees*
US $99–174
*Additional fees subject to change.

Île aux Cerfs Golf Club   *Trou d'Eau Douce, Mauritius*

In golfing terms, the Île aux Cerfs course is certainly not the best course in Mauritius, but it offers visitors a unique experience thanks to its location, picturesque views and dense tropical vegetation. A considerable amount of effort was put in to deliver this gem, which is a feast for all the senses. As Bernhard Langer explained: "I want it to be a game to remember for all who play." The course has also been modified on two occasions, in 2013 and 2014, so it could better suit all types of play. All the holes have a view of the sea, either through vegetation or by being almost on the shore, which is the case for 11 of the 18 holes. This course is distinctive for its carefully positioned bunkers and 20 or so water hazards, four of which are

the size of a small lake. This just amplifies the beauty of the surroundings, as if it was needed, and adds a bit of spice to the round. It is difficult to elect a signature hole at this course, but the short 8th, with a raised tee above a bowl surrounded by mangroves and outcrops of volcanic rock, could well be the one. The fairways are narrow here, so it is well worth starting out with a good stock of balls. A bad driving day can never be ruled out, even in paradise!

Anahita Golf Club *Beau Champ, Mauritius*

Growing grass in the desert is no longer a challenge. Dubai now has 20 or so golf courses, without counting the two courses under construction in Jumeirah, Water and Wind. Water was designed by Vijay Singh, winner of 59 pro trophies. Three golfing masters, Sergio Garcia, Greg Norman and Pete Dye, teamed up to design Wind, which will be in keeping with the purest of links traditions. Once this project is completed, Jumeirah will have almost 10 times more green space than rainy London's Hyde Park! The Majlis, the Emirates Golf Club's flagship (following spread) was the first 18-hole course to emerge from the desert sands, back in 1988. Commissioned by Sheikh Al Maktoum, it is now surrounded by the Nick Faldo Course. The most memorable holes include the par-3 7th, lined by a water hazard along its entire length, and the 18th, where players need to hit their approach over another lake to reach the green. Ernie Els holds the course record at Majlis, having scored 11 under par at the Dubai Desert Classic in 1994.

Established
2009

Par
72

Length
7,706 yards
(7,046 m)

Green fees*
US $107–194
*Additional fees subject to change.

Jumeirah Golf Estates *Dubai, United Arab Emirates*

In Dubai, excessiveness is simply a way of life. The Jumeirah Golf Estates is no exception. The promoters of this gigantic complex, which combines buildings and greens, aim to make it into one of the planet's green paradises, eventually incorporating four courses, named Earth, Fire, Water and Wind. The first two, which opened in 2009 and 2010, are designed by Greg Norman, who needs no introduction. Earth is currently the flagship of this work in progress, which, before being opened to the public, was christened by the pros during the final stage of the European Tour, the Dubai World Championship. It was at that event that it became clear Norman had created a very high-level golf course. Indeed, some players believe that Earth's last four holes represent the toughest mile of golf on the planet. Fire is undoubtedly more manageable for amateurs, especially the back nine, where better players could well find themselves with a few birdie opportunities. But don't be fooled, it is still a very high-level course and aesthetically superb, too. Players at Fire are greeted by links-type surroundings, wind included, despite the waters of the Persian Gulf being less than a dozen miles away. In Dubai, if you want it, you can find it!

Emirates Golf Club *Dubai, United Arab Emirates*

Earmarked to host the 2020 Olympic Games (held in 2021 due to COVID-19), Hirono was completely renovated in the hopes of rediscovering the spirit of Charles H. Alison's original design, which was without a doubt one of his biggest successes. The famous architect designed several courses across Japan, laying the foundations for the incredible success that golf now enjoys across the archipelago, having become the country's number one sport, ahead of sumo wrestling and baseball. The first 18-hole course on Japanese soil dates back to 1903, but golf really took off in the 1950s, following the Japanese team's first victory in a world team championship, at the Canada Cup. The country now has 35,000 driving ranges and 2,500 courses. Hirono lost its original features after being turned into a military base during the Second World War, hence the importance of Martin Ebert's extensive renovation. Despite being a private course, Hirono does allow some visitor access, providing they are accompanied by a member.

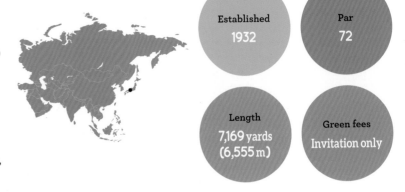

Established
1932

Par
72

Length
7,169 yards
(6,555 m)

Green fees
Invitation only

Hirono Golf Club   *Miki, Hyogo, Japan*

The new lease on life that this most famous of Japanese courses has been given means this 88-year-old course is suddenly bursting with youthful exuberance. In 2019, the club was closed for 10 months to complete renovation work, which led to a good deal of speculation and expectation around the golfing world. What a challenge for the architects and landscapers to work on this gem — the historic host of the biggest international tournaments ever held in Japan! Trees were pruned, as some holes had been choked with branches. Greens were resurfaced, even though they were reputedly magnificent, making the terrain easier to read. Lastly, bunkers were redesigned to give them a more intimidating and

aggressive appearance. Hirono covers 128 acres (52 ha) of sandy ground with an ideal level of undulation and about 130 feet (40 m) of elevation change at most. It sits amid extremely dense, lush vegetation and is bordered to the west by a series of lakes and reservoirs through which six of its holes weave their way. It would be criminally unfair to pick a single iconic hole, but the 13th (above) is worth a special mention. This 166-yard (152 m) par 3 is reminiscent of Golden Bell, Augusta's famous 12th hole, where the ball needs to make it over water and the green is accessed by a small stone bridge. However, connoisseurs of this hole at Hirono, known as Loch Lomond, claim it is even more spectacular.

When Charles H. Alison set eyes on this peninsula combining rolling hills, a wooded plateau and ocher cliffs plunging into Sagami Bay, it was love at first sight! Although there was already an 18-hole course (Oshima, designed by a Japanese architect in Kawana in 1928), it paled in comparison with what Alison came up with for Baron Okura Kishichiro, who owned the land. Here is a high-level course that charges the priciest green fees in the country. There is a very British atmosphere to the surroundings, and not just on the greens. Jackets and trousers are required when on club premises. In Japan, the sport of golf is governed by strict conventions and subject to a great deal of formality. You don't just go to hit a few balls. However, it is also important to find relaxation for both the body and mind. Playing a round takes the whole day, as a lunch break after the front nine is an absolute must, as is a dip in the hot tub once the 18th is done and dusted. And if, to cap it all, Mount Fuji appears through the mist and the resort's 9,000 cherry trees are heavy with blossoms, the enchantment of the place is unparalleled.

Established
1936

Par
72

Length
6,701 yards
(6,127 m)

Green fees*
US $279–405
*Additional fees subject to change.

Kawana Hotel Golf Course (Fuji Course) *Kawana, Shizuoka, Japan*

It comes with a hefty price tag for most visitors, but the traveling golfer can't afford to miss a trip to Japan, where the sport has become a new religion. Having developed into extremely capable players, the Japanese also quickly learned how to strive for excellence when it comes to golf courses, of which this course is the finest example. It offers a unique panorama with an unobstructed view of the Pacific Ocean from the cliffs and Mount Fuji looming in the background. The fairways are enclosed, and the greens are surrounded by vegetation. Players are immersed in nature, which has been an irresistible draw for Tokyo residents, eager to take a break from the hustle and bustle of the city. They also come here

for the back nine, which some believe features the most beautiful holes of golf in Japan. The highlight is the par-5 11th, the longest hole on the course at 568 yards (519 m), with a green facing a tee-shaped lighthouse. The 15th hole is a crazy 437-yard (400 m) downhill ride along an undulating fairway skirting the coastline. It should be said that the ambiance of the place exudes more than a hint of California's Pebble Beach. On the 17th, players need to avoid four deep bunkers to reach the green. These are nicknamed "Alison Bunkers" after the architect who made them one of his hallmarks. What an outing!

Kyle Phillips, the architect behind Kingsbarns, Morfontaine and many other courses, also designed this course at the request of a Korean business magnate who invested enormous sums in the project. Everything about South Cape Owners is outstanding. The setting on a rocky peninsula is remarkable, with sea views from every hole, and the magnificent course overlooks an incredible curved, ultramodern and ultra-luxurious clubhouse. The same futuristic design was chosen for the tea house located near the 15th hole. Every aspect of the course

has been scrutinized in minute detail to ensure tranquility, relaxation and pleasure. Nevertheless, in a country with countless private clubs, it is important to point out that this heaven on Earth is public and open to everyone and suited to all levels of player. The back nine is particularly spectacular, and some holes (especially the 16th) rival those of Cypress Point and Cape Kidnappers in terms of sheer beauty, with a wonderful touch of modernity thrown in for good measure.

Established
2013

Par
72

Length
7,313 yards
(6,687 m)

Green fees*
US $164–306
*Additional fees subject to change.

South Cape Owners Club *Gyeongsangnam-do, South Korea*

It is possible to love both Renaissance painters and contemporary art. The same can be said for golf courses. You can appreciate the history, traditions and charm of the old stonework of St. Andrews but also immensely enjoy discovering the cutting-edge modernity of newer courses. South Cape Owners falls unquestionably into the second category. This very young club (opened in 2013) has its own identity and is far from being a clone of European golf courses. The tees and fairways have been sown with bluegrass, the rough with fescue and the greens with bent grass, creating a subtle nuance of different shades of green across an extremely undulating course. Granite outcrops line some of the fairways as a reminder of the

jagged coastline and cobalt waters of the East China Sea beyond. The course is designed for very high-level golf, as exemplified by the 5th hole, a 533-yard (487 m) par 5 with a double dogleg, first right then left. You can try to approach the flag directly, but it comes with a risk, since the green is positioned on a cliff edge and is heavily protected by four bunkers. On the back nine, the 14th and 16th, two coastal par 3s, confirm the words of site owner Jae Bong Chung: "At South Cape, you are in a special place."

South Cape Owners Club *Gyeongsangnam-do, South Korea*

At the base of Mount Halla-san, South Korea's highest point, standing at 6,388 feet (1,950 m), Nine Bridges blends in with its exceptional setting by respecting the natural environment that surrounds it. Indeed, it is not unusual to come across a wild animal between two greens. The stone, timber and glass clubhouse is a wonder of modern design, with an astonishing atrium held up by columns that, from a distance, look like giant wicker tees. The two courses are punctuated by eight bridges, with a ninth serving a more figurative purpose, symbolizing the link between the club and its members. The Hallasan volcano, a UNESCO World Heritage Site, reveals its majestic slopes in the backdrop. The zen-like calmness of the site is misleading. Players have to make their way through tunnels of volcanic rock and up paths climbing to the edge of the crater. Jeju is in many ways the Hawaii of Asia, becoming a popular destination for Chinese and Japanese tourists.

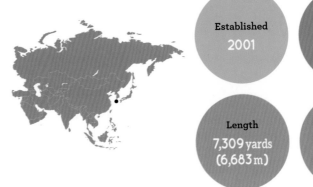

Established
2001

Par
72

Length
7,309 yards
(6,683 m)

Green fees
Private club

Nine Bridges Golf Club *Jeju Island, South Korea*

Tradition meets modernity at Nine Bridges. Despite this being a cliché as well-worn as a green scorched by the summer sun, it nicely sums up the atmosphere here. Although the club might be thought of as young compared to some of its European counterparts, its promoters have succeeded in recreating a unique blend befitting the sport of golf, making this magical site the must-play course in South Korea and perhaps even all of Asia. Inspired by Scottish courses and designed by Golf Plan USA, who are renowned for the quality of their landscaping, this undulating and varied course alternates between long and short holes, offering front and back nines with very different features and surroundings. The part

known as the Creek Course is made up of small streams, bushes and stone walls. The wilder, more European Highland Course has wide fairways, a green perched on an island in a small lake and a bumper crop of bunkers (there are more than 110 in all across the whole course). The beauty and difficulty of this course didn't go unnoticed by the organizers of the professional circuit. Indeed, since 2002, Nine Bridges has regularly hosted LPGA events. As well-known for his swing as for his way with words, former American champion Chi Chi Rodriguez once called this course the "Taj Mahal of golf" because every hole looks like a postcard.

Nine Bridges Golf Club   *Jeju Island, South Korea*

With an entry fee of a million dollars and only 20 or so members at most, Shanqin is without a doubt the world's most select golf club. They say that several architecture firms turned this project down before Bill Coore and Ben Crenshaw took up the mantle of creating a course over very complex terrain featuring cliffs, dunes, subtropical vegetation and elevation changes along a magnificent coastline. Severely damaged by the 2008 tsunami, Shanqin has continued to develop since then, thanks in large part to a new high-speed train line and two nearby airports. The Island of Hainan has become a very popular destination among Chinese billionaires in particular. Dozens of golf courses have opened in recent years, including the impressive Mission Hills Haikou, which has no fewer than 10 courses, one of which is the acclaimed Blackstone Course. It owes its name to the ever-present volcanic rock around its undulating course of 8,530 yards (7,800 m), with an interplay of centuries-old trees, vast lakes, dense jungle and wetland.

Established
2011

Par
72

Length
7,532 yards
(6,887 m)

Green fees
Private club

Shanqin Bay Golf Club   *Wanning, Hainan, China*

Is it any surprise that the world's most exclusive course is an extraordinary place? At least this is what we are led to believe based on accounts from the scrupulously selected guests (only around 10 per year) who get the chance to explore the club and try out its coastal course, celebrated for its topographical variety and the expansiveness of its fairways. Although it is tough to highlight specific holes on a championship-level course that is so consistently high quality, according to (rare) accounts, on the front nine, the par-4 5th and the short par-3 8th are particular standouts. The 5th is both a delight and a challenge, with a fairway wrapped around a reservoir. It ends with a green perched on a crest, which players

need to reach without being able to see it. The 8th hole is nothing less than thrilling. The aim here is to get over a ravine before plunging into a sea of greenery closely bordered by dunes. The back nine is also highly acclaimed, especially the final four holes, which offer a sensational final series with great views over the sea (particularly the 15th). The highlight here is undoubtedly the 16th, a 307-yard (281 m) par 4 with an elevation change of a good 50 feet (about 15 m) between the tee and the green, offering a view over the sea that is truly unforgettable, much like a visit to Shanqin Bay Golf Club as a whole.

The Ayodhya Golf Club claims to be a links course, and yet it doesn't have any of the main features, namely dunes and proximity to the sea. You might therefore be forgiven for thinking that the club management is taking liberties, but the thing is, there aren't really any rules governing what makes a links course a links. As surprising as it may seem for a sport as standardized as golf, there is no official authority in charge of granting such a title, not even the Royal & Ancient, the ultimate arbiter of all things golf. So what is a links course? It is a course on a coast that runs along a strip of undulating land or amid dunes, just as the very first British golf courses were back in the 17th century. The playing area is also in complete harmony with nature. At first, only courses in the British Isles could be considered links. Over time, this historic concept, which carries with it a certain sporting philosophy, was gradually exported overseas.

Established
2007

Par
72

Length
7,639 yards
(6,985 m)

Green fees
Private club

Ayodhya Links Golf Club   *Ayutthaya, Thailand*

Although the democratization of golf has been well underway for 30 years or so, there are still some small pockets of resistance here and there. What gives the sport its charm is that, despite its changes, it maintains a subtly antiquated touch. The Ayodhya Links, an hour's drive north of Bangkok, is a perfect illustration of this. This little gem is only open to its own members, who are handpicked from Thailand's high society. Based on plans from the design firm Thomson and Perrett, this course is the handiwork of Pitak Intrawityanunt, one of the project's founders and the club's current chairman. Its distinctive feature is the ever-present water, to such an extent that you could be forgiven for thinking you were playing on a coastal course. With rolling fairways, slick greens, ingenious bunkers (79 in total) and a wide variety of holes, this course is not just an undeniable aesthetic and technical triumph (the course was raised by about 13 feet [4 m] after terrible floods in 2011!) but also a very high-level course that requires plenty of long drives. It stretches nearly 4 1/2 miles (7 km) in total from the back tees. Ayodhya Links can also pride itself on its truly sustainable approach, since it refrains from using any chemicals in the upkeep of this verdant paradise, which just goes to show that luxury and environmental commitments are not mutually exclusive.

While many great champions happily turn to course design at the end of their playing career, Ernie Els decided to do both at the same time, and he achieved equal success both on and off the greens! Nicknamed the "Big Easy" because of the metronomic rhythm of his swing, he won four Major titles (the US Open in 1994 and 1997 and the British Open in 2002 and 2012) and claimed 71 pro victories. After just 10 years on the circuit, the South African champion founded an architecture firm in partnership with renowned American designer Greg Letsche, who earned his stripes alongside Pete Dye and later Jack Nicklaus. Els Design has created or renovated 20 or so courses worldwide, six of which have hosted pro circuit events. With another 10 or so projects in the works, Els Design really is in full swing. This has also enabled its owner to extend his time on the circuit: at 51, Els competed in more than 20 tournaments during the 2019 season.

Established
1992

Par
72

Length
6,760 yards
(6,181m)

Green fees*
US $90
*Additional fees
subject to change.

Els Club Teluk Datai *Kedah, Langkawi, Malaysia*

Like many players, Ernie Els turned his attention to course design, founding his own company in 2000. The South African champion's firm has designed some 20 courses, four of which bear his name, including Els Club Teluk Datai, located on the Malaysian island of Langkawi in the Andaman Sea. In 2014, in the exceptional setting of a 10-million-year-old rainforest, Els and his team set to work on a course considered too short and too narrow in its original version, which was designed by Ted Parslow in 1992. The number of awards the course has received since it reopened would suggest that Els Design's efforts have been a tremendous success. The distinctive characteristic of this course, which blends coastal and jungle holes,

is the absence of bunkers, which would be very complicated to maintain given the location's abundant rain and humidity. However, this decision in no way affects the quality of the course, which is open to all. According to accounts, there is no end to the surprises, with a number of holes featuring tricky doglegs. In this setting, there are plenty of distractions, starting with the majestic views from the coastal holes, not to mention the frequent intrusions of macaques and other small monkeys found in the region. Even in the low season, you are never alone at Teluk Datai.

Located a stone's throw from Sydney on the tip of the entrance to Botany Bay, "La Perouse," as the club is also called, will soon be celebrating its 100th anniversary. It is a location with a long and colorful history. The 17th hole is just above the source from which Captain Cook's crew replenished their supplies back in 1770. A few years later, Louis XVI sent the ship *La Pérouse* on a voyage of scientific exploration, and it dropped anchor in the same place before the first European colonists settled here. A military area until the end of the First World War, this barren moorland was then earmarked for the creation of this links course, but it continued to be shared with the army until after the Second World War. Even then, connections remained strong between the club and military authorities, especially when it came to the club's management. The course was significantly modernized in the 1980s and 1990s, but the original design, created by Alister MacKenzie (with finishing touches from Eric Apperly), has remained unchanged.

Established
1928

Par
72

Length
6,830 yards
(6,245 m)

Green fees
Upon request

New South Wales Golf Club *Sydney, New South Wales, Australia*

The New South Wales Golf Club is considered to be Australia's toughest course. The second hole, with its minuscule green, is just a taste of the many joys to come. What distinguishes this course is the varied orientation of its holes. If the wind changes, it is hard to get your bearings, just like on British links. These conditions can easily make you lose your cool, but they are also a great challenge for hardened players. The same can be said for the terrain, which is relatively undulating throughout and combined with reputedly ultra-quick greens. The series of holes 5, 6 and 7 is considered by many to be the course's best sequence. Once again, whether northerly or southerly, the wind is liable to completely change the situation and your choice of club, especially on the world-famous par-3 6th (above), which is the closest to the ocean and has a back tee perched on a rocky outcrop. At New South Wales Golf Club, where nothing is easy, it is often the diabolical and magnificent 6th that really spoils the party. It is made very clear to players coming here for the first time that anyone returning to the clubhouse having played a round that's five or six shots off their handicap can be very proud.

Alex Russel, Australian hero of the First World War and winner of the 1924 Australian Open, was tasked with devising a second course for the splendid and very select RMGC, located in Melbourne's southeastern suburbs. The East course, modernized by Tom Doak, is said to be less difficult that its big brother due to its shallow bunkers, flatter topography and smaller greens. But don't be fooled, the East is still an extremely high-level and equally iconic course, in particular the last four holes. The 17th and 18th are used to close the Composite course, which is a mix of the two courses. However, the highlight of the East course's final series is unquestionably the 16th, which American Ben Crenshaw, two-time Augusta winner, described as "the most beautiful par 3" he had ever seen. At 165 yards (151 m) long, this visual wonder is protected by an army of seven bunkers.

Established
1891

Par
72

Length
6,646 yards
(6,077 m)

Green fees
Invitation only

Royal Melbourne Golf Club *Melbourne, Victoria, Australia*

It is fitting that one of the world's most popular and prestigious golf courses should be located in the great sporting nation of Australia. The Royal Melbourne Golf Club, with over a century of history and two courses, the West (1926; above) and the East (1931; following spread), attracts champions and enthusiasts alike from across the world, enticing them to play Down Under. This double delight was designed by the masters Alister MacKenzie (West) and Alex Russell (East). These two courses were then used to create a third, known as the "Composite," which combines 12 holes from the West and 6 from the East. It was devised in 1959, when the club was chosen to host the World Cup. Since then, it has been reused

on numerous occasions — with a few modifications – for various professional competitions, including the Australian Open 16 times. The West course is based on a philosophy of excellence, one of the guiding principles of Alister MacKenzie, who is also known for his masterpieces at Augusta and Cypress Point, two other golfing meccas. According to MacKenzie, "The course should be so interesting that even the plus man is constantly stimulated to improve his game in attempting shots he has hitherto been unable to play." With slick greens, devilishly positioned bunkers, doglegs and blind approaches, players can't afford to relax at any point on the course, especially when the north wind is a factor.

Royal Melbourne Golf Club *Melbourne, Victoria, Australia*

Off the beaten track in the north of King Island, in the Bass Strait between mainland Australia and Tasmania, Cape Wickham is in keeping with the purest of Scottish or Irish links traditions. American Mike DeVries and Australian Darius Oliver designed a course that harnesses the incredible potential offered by the coastline, which would likely feature many more golf clubs if only it wasn't so remote. After a 45-minute car journey from the island's main town of Currie, the imposing white granite lighthouse built in 1861 looms into view. The place has a sinister reputation for being the site of countless shipwrecks, whose survivors little by little populated the island. The course, the ever-present wind, the bunkers, the tall grass (home to venomous snakes) and sea views from every hole mean that there is never a dull moment at Cape Wickham, and players need to constantly think about their strategy. Once your round is over and your clubs are safely back in their bag, there is nothing left to do but settle down and enjoy the island's specialty: crayfish pie.

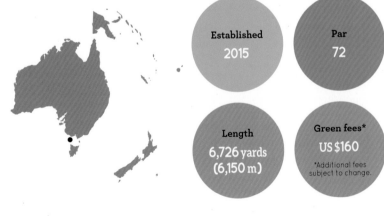

Established
2015

Par
72

Length
6,726 yards
(6,150 m)

Green fees*
US $160
*Additional fees
subject to change.

Cape Wickham Golf Links *King Island, Australia*

You don't end up on King Island by chance. But for anyone who is into golf, it is worth making the trip to Cape Wickham Links, which in just a few short years has become a course cherished by specialists, as attested by its regular appearance in international rankings. Lovers of shoreline golf will be in their element on this 100% coastal course with extremely varied topography. The work of the designers has received glowing reviews, especially when it comes to the first three holes, which offer a superb and deceptively tricky starting sequence (in particular the par-4 1st) — a sign of the difficulties to come. It goes without saying that the wind plays a leading role on this course, whose flagship hole is the 582-yard (532 m) par-5 15th,

with its green situated at the base of the 157-foot (48 m) high lighthouse, famed for being Australia's tallest. The entertainment lasts right until the end, since the 18th, a 433-yard (396 m) par 4, is also a unique hole. The beach along its entire length is an integral part of the playing area, which players need to negotiate. If you can reach it from your drive, then you are in a good position to land on the very narrow green with your next shot. In a certain sense, Cape Wickham has the biggest bunker in the world!

Before the greens and the fairways, there was nothing but dunes and fields of potatoes lining Anderson Bay. A first course, Barnbougle, was built on these stretches of sand and was joined in 2010 by Lost Farm (following spread), a course with... 20 holes! It takes its name from the area where lost cattle used to seek refuge. Despite being neighbors, these two courses have markedly different characteristics. The dunes at Lost Farm are steeper and more spectacular, and the two extra holes provide an added touch of originality: the 13th, initially designed as a replacement hole, and the 18th, a very short par 3 near the clubhouse. The 5th hole is reputed to be the course's best. It's a par 4 where the biggest rewards can be gained by hitting over a dune to reach the right side of the fairway. Once your round is done, it's time to head off to explore the vineyards of the Tamar Valley, since Tasmania is also highly acclaimed for its exquisite cabernet sauvignon.

Established
2004

Par
71

Length
6,724 yards
(6,148 m)

Green fees*
US $80
*Additional fees
subject to change.

Barnbougle Links Golf Resort (The Dunes) *Bridport, Tasmania, Australia*

Despite being well and truly in the southern hemisphere, reminders of the north abound. First of all, the name, Barnbougle, is as Scottish as you can get and was chosen by the owner, who arrived from Edinburgh in the 19th century. The course is a true British-style links with wild fairways and gusty winds that can drive players mad, making it what is generally accepted to be the most coastal golf course in the whole of Australia. The two designers, American Tom Doak and Australian Mike Clayton, are both known for taking a great deal of inspiration from... British courses! And then, of course, you have the dunes, which give the course its undulations and special green and golden vegetation consisting of tall grasses and extremely dense bushes — just another hazard for players to be wary of. The Dunes course at Barnbougle features the biggest and, undoubtedly, the deepest bunker in the southern hemisphere, a huge challenge on the 4th hole and a giant from whose clutches it is hard to escape. Known for the breadth of its fairways, this course is also renowned for its greens, with steep slopes and varied undulations. Some players, no doubt frustrated by their score, claim that "they are no quicker than an old shag carpet." The 5th hole at the Dunes is a tribute to the famous Punch Bowl, the legendary 9th hole at the Royal Liverpool Golf Club, harking back to the northern hemisphere once more.

Barnbougle Links Golf Resort (Lost Farm) *Bridport, Tasmania, Australia*

It was a very different kind of green treasure that led the Maoris to explore the region of Queenstown in the center of the South Island: *pounamu*, a sacred stone similar to jade, often called greenstone, has become one of the emblems of New Zealand. Europeans colonized the area in the 1860s, during the gold rush. Queenstown has now become the "adventure capital of the world." The nearby Kawarau suspension bridge, 141 feet (43 m) above the river below, is the world's very first bungee-jumping site. Since golf is an adventure too, various courses have emerged at the foot of the Remarkables, a mountain range overlooking Queenstown. Beyond Jack's Point, the Queenstown Golf Club (following spread) is without a doubt the most picturesque, with its unique peninsula location. Water, which literally surrounds the course, is also a key feature of the 5th hole, where players need to drive over a lake if they hope to score par.

Established
2008

Par
72

Length
6,986 yards
(6,388 m)

Green fees*
US $59–150
*Additional fees subject to change.

Jack's Point Golf Course *Kawarau Falls, New Zealand*

Playing golf against a backdrop of mountains plunging into the blue water of Lake Wakatipu is a memory that will forever stay with anyone who has been to Jack's Point. On land that did not necessarily lend itself naturally to the creation of a golf course, architect John Darby, in collaboration with Brett Thomson, designed a magnificent course full of surprises, thanks largely to the diversity of its topography. The course is replete with bush, slick greens, uphill and downhill sections, fescue grass fairways, rocky outcrops and stone walls — a reminder of the farm and cattle that occupied this land during centuries gone by. The choice of clubs here is crucial for anyone looking to post a decent score. The picture-postcard 5th and 8th holes are the most spectacular, and the gently sloping par-3 7th is also worth a special mention, with its panoramic view of the unforgettable lake. Holes 9 through 13 weave their way between swamplands on the way back to the clubhouse and, despite all being relatively short par 3s and 4s, are all distinct from one another. Jack's Point has five different tees, allowing all levels of player to enjoy their round. In terms of the surroundings, you'll be sure to leave with a smile on your face, regardless of how many birdies you get.

Queenstown Golf Club *Queenstown, New Zealand*

You would be forgiven for thinking that the dunes and fairways had been sculpted by nature, but you'd be wrong. It took Tom Doak two years to shape the land to perfection after removing several acres of pine forest. Therein lies the magic of Tara Iti! At the end of the track that serves as a rudimentary road, a simple wooden fence marks the entrance to the club. The only thing showy about this club is its natural beauty. Wherever you are, you never lose sight of the ocean and the vast spit of white sand stretching the length of the course. Te Arai beach is renowned for being a top surfing spot. For the Maoris, this is the place where the land and sky meet. When they sold these sacred lands to American billionaire Richard Kayne, they demanded that the site be treated with respect. Kayne plans to build two more courses on neighboring land to enable the club to open up to more people. This will be trickier to achieve, since such plans could threaten the tara iti, an endangered species of tern.

Established
2015

Par
71

Length
6,850 yards
(6,264 m)

Green fees
Invitation only

Tara Iti Golf Club *Northland, New Zealand*

There is a debate raging among those golfers lucky enough to have played in New Zealand: Which of the courses designed by Tom Doak is the best, Cape Kidnappers or Tara Iti? One way of settling it would be to say that Cape Kidnappers is more spectacular, while golfing purists tend to prefer Tara Iti, a shoreline links located a little more than an hour north of Auckland. The extremely sandy ground has been covered in fescue from tee to green on every hole, giving the course a uniform elegance. All the holes offer a view over the southern Pacific Ocean and the islands facing the course. The course's cunningly varied topography (with bowls, hills and dunes) means that players need to constantly be on their guard,

especially on the wondrous sea-facing 444-yard (406 m) par-4 3rd. This hole is played completely blind, since the sunken green is around a bend and concealed by a dune. A special mention should go to the uphill 13th hole, with its green located at the highest point on the course, and the par-5 18th, with a fairway that is surrounded by sand and starts off wide before tapering as it nears the flag. The clubhouse is located at the foot of the green, so onlookers might add a little extra pressure onto players' shoulders, but nailing a long putt despite the tension makes it all worthwhile!

Tara Iti Golf Club *Northland, New Zealand*

Located in the north of the wondrous Bay of Islands, one of New Zealand's most stunning bays populated by dolphins, Kauri Cliffs was designed to give players the most spectacular views possible. And since there's a rule limiting the number of players on the course to 24, they get to feel even more privileged! This part of Northland is a popular resort area, renowned for diving, especially around the wreck of the *Rainbow Warrior*. After being sunk while moored near Auckland in 1985 by the French secret services, the former Greenpeace flagship was moved to the seabed off the Cavalli Islands more than 65 feet (20 m) below the surface. Over time, coral has developed in the hull, providing fish and moray eels with the perfect habitat. The New Zealand coast was also one of the first meeting places between Maoris and Europeans, at the start of the 19th century. It was at Waitangi that the representatives of the crown and the Maori chiefs signed a treaty of the same name, officially making New Zealand a British colony.

Established
2001

Par
72

Length
7,151 yards
(6,539 m)

Green fees*
US $335
*Additional fees subject to change.

Kauri Cliffs Golf Course *Northland, New Zealand*

This is a new, unmissable course for any golfer visiting the land of the Kiwis. When asked about this course, PGA champion Brandt Snedeker, number 4 in the world in 2013, said that "Kauri Cliffs is Pebble Beach on steroids!" That is quite the compliment given that the Californian links course, host of the US Open on six occasions, is one of the world's must-play golf courses. Owned by American billionaire Julian Robertson, who fell in love with New Zealand, Kauri Cliffs is the handiwork of David Harman, who spent two years creating it. The course was then slightly revised by Rees Jones in 2014. Of the 18 holes, 15 have a panoramic view over the Pacific, and six of these holes plunge straight into the waves below. The

4th, where players need to find a path between bunkers and a wide ravine, is considered by many to be one of the best par 5s in the world. The 5th hole, a leap of faith over cliffs, is enough to make anyone break out in a cold sweat. The 16th hole receives a lot of plaudits. It's a downhill par 4 where the gusty wind pushes the ball. The admittedly high green fee notwithstanding, Kauri Cliffs is also known for being a course suited to players of all levels, with five different tees available and broader-than-average greens. There is no reason why this outstanding course should be reserved for the big shots!

Cape Kidnappers is one of those slightly hidden locations that you would love to keep secret. A few miles outside the charming art deco town of Napier, this tip of land owes its name to the attempted kidnapping of a member of Captain Cook's crew by the Maoris. This wilderness is a haven for golfers but also for northern gannets, seabirds that nest in the side of the cliffs in the thousands during the summer months. Players get closest to them on the 15th and 16th holes, where the birds' distinctive calls mix with the noise of the gusting wind. They pay

no mind to wayward golf balls during their tireless aerial displays, much like the sheep grazing in the neighboring fields. Two hours from Cape Kidnappers, Wairakei — another course where players are accompanied by constant birdsong — rivals its neighbor, the Kinloch Club, renowned for being one of Jack Nicklaus's best designs of all time. Despite being far from the sea, this extremely challenging, undulating course that favors a strong short game bears a striking resemblance to British links.

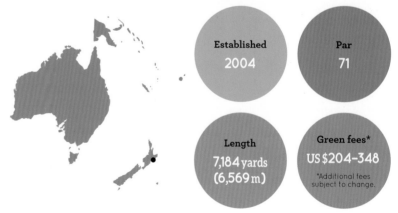

Established
2004

Par
71

Length
7,184 yards
(6,569 m)

Green fees*
US $204–348
*Additional fees
subject to change.

200

Cape Kidnappers *Hawke's Bay, New Zealand*

This course is the embodiment of New Zealand itself: wild and wonderful, breathtaking even, with a unique end-of-the-world atmosphere. Cape Kidnappers is also a course you have to work to get to. The trip takes a good 20 minutes of driving along a track between the road and clubhouse through fields of grazing cows and sheep. Designed by Tom Doak, one of the most highly respected architects in golf worldwide, this links course of crests, cliff-edge slopes — 460 feet (140 m) above the sea — and six holes facing out into the southern Pacific Ocean will delight players of all levels. The course requires players to be adaptable, due to the changeable and unpredictable weather conditions, and, above all, accurate. This

is certainly the case for the pencil-thin 650-yard (594 m) par-5 15th hole (following spread), where a perfectly straight drive is a must. Although good golfers never tire of reminding us that you shouldn't get distracted by the view, it is impossible not to be in this place, especially at the 16th tee, which is raised and provides an even better panorama of Hawke's Bay. At Cape Kidnappers, the exceptional scenery is an integral part of the experience, even if it means your scorecard ends up with two or three extra shots. Fortunately, players return to dry land for the last two holes, giving them a chance to get their breath back on the way to the clubhouse.

Cape Kidnappers *Hawke's Bay, New Zealand*

INDEX

The author would like to thank Guillaume Baraise for his wise and valuable advice.

IMAGE CREDITS

AFP: 142–143, 146–147, 160–161

Alamy Images: 92–93, 114–115, 126–127

Alexis Orloff: 58–59, 60–61

Ayodhya Links: 178–179

Casa de Campo: 138–139

Christian Segui: 62–63

Corales Golf Course: 136–137

Cruden Bay Golf Club: 18–19

Diamante Dunes Golf Course: 132–133

Gary Lisbon: 26–27, 30–31, 36–37, 48–49, 106–107, 118–119, 120–121, 134–135, 144–145, 164–165, 166–167, 172–173, 174–175, 176–177, 184–185, 186–187, 188–189, 194–195, 204–205, 206–207

Getty Images: 28–29, 52–53, 64–65, 66–67, 162–163

Gord Wylie: 94–95

Iain Lowe: 12–13

Jacob Sjöman: 22–23, 38–39, 40–41, 54–55, 56–57, 80–81, 82–83, 84–85, 86–87, 88–89, 90–91, 140–141, 156–157, 190–191, 192–193, 198–199, 200–201, 202–203

Jason Livy: 50–51

Joann Dost: 168–169, 170–171

Koninklijke Haagsche Country Club: 74–75

Lahinch Golf Club: 32–33, 34–35

Mike Centioli: 14–15, 20–21, 96–97, 98–99, 100–101, 102–103, 116–117, 130–131

NSW Golf Club: 182–183

Paul Severn: 8–9, 10–11, 16–17, 42–43, 76–77, 78–79, 110–111, 112–113, 122–123, 124–125, 128–129, 150–151, 152–153, 154–155, 158–159, 180–181

Real Club Valderrama: 68–69

Shutterstock: 24–25, 70–71, 104–105, 148–149, 196–197

Stefan von Stengel: 72–73

Stuart Morley: 44–45, 46–47

SilverRock Resort: 108–109